THE CORPORATE LIFE SURVIVAL GUIDE

Randy Zinn

SOR Press
GAITHERSBURG, MARYLAND

Randy Zinn/SOR Press
Gaithersburg, Maryland
www.randy-zinn.com

Publisher's Note: Any names, characters, or places have been changed to protect anonymity. Any resemblance to actual people, living or dead, or to businesses, companies, events, institutions, or locales is coincidental.

Publisher's Cataloging-In-Publication Data
(Prepared by The Donohue Group, Inc.)

Names: Zinn, Randy, author.
Title: The corporate life survival guide / Randy Zinn.
Description: 1st ed. | Gaithersburg, Maryland : SOR Press, [2021]
Identifiers: ISBN 9781953643049 (paperback)
 | ISBN 9781953643056 (hardcover)
 | ISBN 9781953643070 (mobi/Kindle)
 | ISBN 9781953643094 (ePub)
Subjects: LCSH: Business etiquette. | Corporate culture.
Classification: LCC HF5389 .Z56 2021 (print) |
 LCC HF5389 (ebook) |
 DDC 395.52--dc23

Contents

ACKNOWLEDGEMENTS

Special thanks to Logan Russell and Daniela Zorrilla

Edited by Kathy Macfarlane

Cover design by Damonza

Introduction

Like most areas in life, the corporate world has many opportunities for success or failure. We can enter it believing that we only need to do well at our job's duties, overlooking the myriad of workplace politics issues that can arise in the meantime. This book is designed to help navigate these issues before any trouble arises, and chart a course out of difficulties if they are already upon us. But it is always easier to evade a mistake than to resolve it. We all make them, and the wisest among us learn from the missteps of others.

I wrote this book for anyone just entering the corporate world or within a few years of starting, but it can benefit also those with more experience. Many books exist on this subject for managers or executives, and while they can also benefit from this book, the target audience is non-managers.

The corporate world has sometimes been compared to high school, but it can be more challenging for two reasons. First, tension between us and someone else can cost us our job, which has real-world financial consequences and stress. Second, our coworkers are adults who we could expect to be above high schoolish behavior, but they sometimes aren't. The bullies of youth may become coworkers who have not reformed. We don't expect to be on the receiving end of bullying and other negative behaviors, but we might be. Not everyone has great people skills or the ability to gracefully resolve conflict. This setting can surprise newcomers, but this book is designed to help you avoid these unpleasant experiences.

Avoidance is a skill of survival and that's the primary intent of this book.

The chapters can be read in any order. Those facing a specific issue can skip to the related section, though the guidance is best absorbed *before* any trouble starts.

Where to Start

I began my career as a software developer in the late 1990s, knowing little to nothing about the corporate world in which I would spend the next two decades. I have been a direct employee, a contractor, a consultant through my firm, and done contract-to-hire. I have created software and the corresponding documentation for my employers/clients or *their* clients, who are sometimes local governments, commercial clients, and a non-profit, but are usually federal government agencies like NASA, the State Department, the White House, the Army, Navy, Marines, IRS, and more.

I hold Microsoft certifications, but my degree is a Bachelor of Music in classical guitar, Magna cum Laude, from Catholic University in D.C.; I was originally a music composition major. Under another name, I've released multiple albums of my music and a classical guitar CD, with me engineering them in my studio and releasing on my record label. I have also published several novels, memoirs, and non-fiction books via my publishing company and its imprints. I live with my son and daughter in the Maryland suburbs north of D.C.

On a more personal note, I've overcome many issues in life, including being Learning Disabled, having Inattentive ADHD, speech problems, a devastating injury to both arms, and more. I know how to survive, even thrive, in tough conditions.

About Me

I began my career as a software developer in the late 1990s, knowing little to nothing about the corporate world in which I would spend the next two decades. I have been a direct employee, a contractor, a consultant through my firm, and done contract-to-hire. I have created software and the corresponding documentation for my employers/clients or *their* clients, who are sometimes local governments, commercial clients, and a non-profit, but are usually federal government agencies like NASA, the State Department, the White House, the Army, Navy, Marines, IRS, and more.

I hold Microsoft certifications, but my degree is a Bachelor of Music in classical guitar, Magna cum Laude, from Catholic University in D.C.; I was originally a music composition major. Under another name, I've released multiple albums of my music and a classical guitar CD, with me engineering them in my studio and releasing on my record label. I have also published several novels, memoirs, and non-fiction books via my publishing company and its imprints. I live with my son and daughter in the Maryland suburbs north of D.C.

On a more personal note, I've overcome many issues in life, including being Learning Disabled, having Inattentive ADHD, speech problems, a devastating injury to both arms, and more. I know how to survive, even thrive, in tough conditions.

Disclaimers

All recommendations, including those in this book, must be carefully considered as to whether they apply to our situation. What works for one person may not work for another, given our differing personalities and life skills. We also have different professions, and work in different parts of the world, though much of the advice is universal. This is why I explain the underlying concepts rather than provide a script for exactly what to say or do in situations.

Throughout the book are anecdotes from my two decades of experience. These are present to highlight the reason for the suggested advice. All of them are featured in more detail in my memoirs, *Adventures in Opposite Land*, *Corporate Hell: A Memoir*, and *Consulting Hell: A Memoir*. The examples are often about things going wrong, and can paint a picture of corporate life being more challenging than it really is, but this is akin to watching the news, which mostly shows negative items because people react to that. That can also paint an unrealistic picture of what life is like. It seems worse when I put twenty years of issues into a book that can be read in hours. The realty is that in most cases, we will not frequently encounter issues. Also, in many cases, the same person was responsible for 2-3 of the anecdotes; difficult coworkers are not quite as common as this book may suggest.

Free Book

Subscribers to my newsletter receive a free eBook of *Adventures in Opposite Land (The Memoir Shorts, 1)*. Among the stories is one about my first job after college, an early foray into the corporate world that this book explores in more depth.

Visit http://www.randy-zinn.com/newsletter

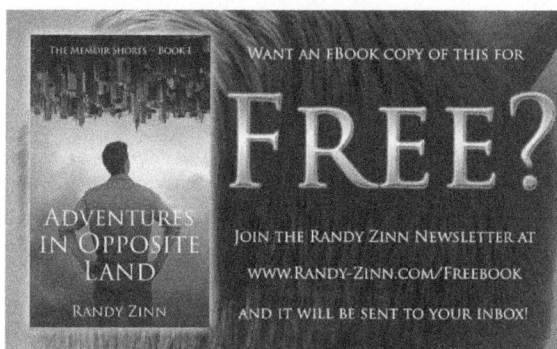

Part One

On the Job

CHAPTER ONE

Mistakes to Avoid

Not all mistakes are created equal. Some are more obvious. Other may get us into trouble. And a few might get us disliked. But all can be avoided more easily with awareness.

Going Over Someone's Head

Most of us know not to "go over someone's head," meaning bypassing someone and going to their manager. Even the appearance of this can get us into trouble. And sometimes it happens by accident. This is especially easy when our manager's supervisor is interacting with us and a subject that we should discuss with our supervisor instead comes up. The trick here is just not to talk about certain things, such as about promotions, vacations, work hours and schedule, or new opportunities at work. Anything related to changing our employment details is off-limits.

This can be true even if someone other than HR or our boss is giving us updates on those details and we have questions. It's natural to ask, but be careful. If we're told details are changing and we would like them not to, mentioning that to this person, if they are not our manager, can be seen as going over our manager's head. We may even be asked if we have questions, to which we may want to respond that we don't right now and we'll ask our boss if so, and thank them.

Sometimes our manager is replaced because the company has promoted ours. Now there is someone in between us and our old supervisor, with whom we may have a great relationship. And a history. It can sometimes be tempting to reach out to them, but be careful. If it is about changing employment details, we cannot. An additional scenario is our actual manager being in one physical location, but their manager, or another one, is at our location and it is therefore more convenient to talk to them about various items. Project details or matters relating to the location (such as dealing with the client if we are at the client site) can be done this way. But again, anything relating to changing our employment details should only be discussed with our direct manager.

We can be tempted to go over a peer's head as well, to their boss. But if we are having an issue with them and cannot resolve it directly, we must talk to our own manager, not theirs. Hopefully ours will intervene on our behalf, as this is what they are supposed to help us with. But many will not because doing so means telling another manager that their staff member is not measuring up. Some people do not have the diplomacy to do this. Or they don't get along with that supervisor and see this as another tension-filled moment in waiting. It can also seem like we threw the person under the bus to our boss, who is now doing it to that person, too, to theirs. But we have the right, even the obligation, to inform our manager and let them try to resolve it. Ultimately, it is not our job to make someone else do theirs unless we are their manager. If the person is holding us up, we document that in writing to our supervisor and let things play out.

Anecdote Time

Before my software development career, I worked in customer service, where I gained a duty no one else had—reviewing CDs we sold and writing sales info for other staff to use. The extra work conflicted with my normal duties. With my manager absent from the room, the Chief Operating Officer gave me grief about the impact on those duties, so I admitted it stretched me too thin. She pressured me to get it done, and I offered to come in early to accomplish this; I was a part-time employee, and they sometimes made me stay late to do similar work. The next day, HR called me into a meeting and admonished me for supposedly requesting to be made a full-time employee to the COO and going over my manager's head to do it. Astonished, I told them I had done no such thing, but they didn't believe me. My boss was furious. She wasn't the only one. One way to mitigate this is to be clear what we are asking and *not* asking, reducing the chance for misunderstanding. We have all been guilty of "I know what I meant" syndrome, so make sure they know what you mean.

Throwing Under the Bus

Getting another person in trouble with management arises when someone is not performing their job duties or when they make a mistake. One question is whether it is our responsibility to call attention to these. And the answer is yes, but only to our supervisor, not theirs or anyone else (that would be "going over their head;" see the previous section). An exception would also be something that we should tell HR, such as sexual harassment, but that isn't really "throwing under the bus" because it is more serious.

What do we do if our manager does not intervene, or doing so cannot resolve an issue? Document that we alerted our boss to the issue (i.e., email about it). That is often all we can do. The reason we want to do this is to show we have made an attempt at getting a resolution through the proper channels. The other person's failure may come back to us, such as the case when them not doing their job prevents us from doing ours. We will be asked what we did to mitigate this, and bringing it to our manager's attention is the answer. A side effect here is that we may now throw our manager under the bus to someone else if that other person is the one asking why this has not been resolved.

But we have a right to defend ourselves if blame for the project failure is looking to be aimed at us, even when this blame is not explicit but implied. We must strive to sound professional and show that we tried to resolve the issue. It's critical to not come across as emotional, resentful, defensive, or vengeful. Be aware that no matter our approach to this, the person whose failure we have brought attention to may resent it. They can feel that they've been thrown under the bus regardless of how we handle it.

One approach is lightheartedness and appearing like we don't mind the issue in the least. This prevents us from seeming judgmental, and this is important. Judging is a form of attitude, as is frustration. There is a difference between, "My part is done and I'm waiting for John Doe's input so I can finish," and, "John Doe is two days late and no matter what I say to him, he just doesn't do his job." If we watch our tone, word choice, and emotions, we can avoid this mistake.

Showing Attitude

Having an "attitude," meaning a negative one, is a significant offense in the corporate world, where we are expected to show only positive emotions. We must strive to not show it, or better yet, to not feel it or have it. There is an assumption that we're mature, dignified professionals, and adults. Showing attitude can be taken as proof we are not, and therefore that we don't fit into this setting. This is unrealistic, because work and the people therein are often frustrating, as is life. But that doesn't mean we're allowed to show our frustration. We must rise about it, especially when someone else has failed to do so.

One troubling aspect is that trying to stifle an attitude rarely works. It comes out anyway in subtle ways, like tone, body language, or word choice. This is still enough to upset people. One solution is a perspective about what is causing our viewpoint, because understanding the attitude we've developed can help us find ways to resolve it. How to do so is too broad a subject for this book, but if we are prone to developing an attitude, it is wise to understand why this is so and mitigate it.

Trying to lose attitude by adopting indifference is a possibility that can be problematic. It can make us lose the attitude but stop caring about the job or even our careers. More useful is trying not to take anything personally, especially when it *is* personal. No one is out to get us, even when it seems they are. Frustration is best met with a silent sigh of acceptance. Resentment is a known love-killer noy only in intimate relationships, but also in professional ones, and we should prevent it from taking root in us.

We can have an attitude for reasons that have nothing to do with work. Personal troubles are an unfortunate part of life, but many people falsely assume that our current location causes our mindset of the moment. This leads to an assumption that a display of attitude on our part means we are unhappy with our employment, a problem that some can solve for us by termination. This is one of the many dangers that attitude poses.

We often feel that having an attitude is justified. This is irrelevant. If ten things have caused the chip on our shoulder, those ten put together are not as big of an offense as having an attitude. This is so true that if someone ever uses the word "attitude" to describe us at our job, it may be prudent to polish the resume.

All of this applies to being in a foul mood, as they see this as attitude. In that sense, being in a bad mood at work is not acceptable and we should do whatever we can to remove it before arriving, or take a quick break to get past it.

Anecdote Time

I once fell out of favor with a Vice President, to whom my manager reported. One day, the VP sent me and a coworker an email asking who was best able to answer the client's question. I knew nothing about the project, which was solely my coworker's, so the question surprised me. I responded that he was the best one. The next day, my boss called me into a meeting and said, "the VP is not happy about your attitude." Startled, I asked what she was talking about and learned that the VP had seen my response as dismissive and unhelpful. My manager soon understood the truth of the situation and we were "good." It is always best to clear up misunderstandings like this as soon as we know of them.

Seeming Like We Don't Want to Help

We have our job duties and others have theirs. This suggests that certain things are "not our job." This is a phrase to avoid saying at work even if it's true, or we think it is. A company has a mission, and while we are there to do our part with a specific job function, we also support the company's overall plans. This can mean "taking one for the team" by doing something outside our normal tasks. But this is not something to seek unless we want to. It usually comes up when a manager asks us to deal with it. Saying no to a supervisor is unwise, and "that's not my job" is a version of this that is worse because we're also correcting (chastising?) someone with more power. Our only recourse is to do it, like it or not. And don't grumble either.

If it happens once, just move on after the task is complete. It becomes more of a problem when we are repeatedly asked, especially if there is a theme that suggests our responsibilities are being changed long term, or we are being groomed for a position that does not align with our goals for that job or our career. This may warrant a conversation with the manager who is asking us to perform extra duties. Find out what their plans are for you, but you can let them know if this is not a path you desire.

If management does indeed intend an unwelcome change, we should learn all that we can about it before deciding that it is not a path suited to us. Some of us who are new to our careers may be more willing to adapt to unexpected changes, but those who are more experienced, more certain, or more determined to pursue a specific course may resist such changes. It is important to assess the long-term ramifications and whether the unexpected is actually a negative or another opportunity for success. Do not be too hasty.

But if we have decided the change is not in our best interests, we may need to start discreetly looking for another job. And this is one reason to go along with the changes, whether we have decided to leave or not. Staying but grumbling is not a great solution.

Anecdote Time

A company hired me with the stated goal of training me as a SharePoint developer, but once I was on board, they had me train myself as well as others they hired after me. They then assigned each of those people to development projects while they left me behind as the trainer. I was not okay with this and asked when I would get a project, too, but none came. It worsened when they decided I was to become a SharePoint administrator. A talk with my manager resolved the situation, and they soon put me on a coding effort. Don't be afraid to realign your goals with the company's if they diverge.

Stepping on People's Toes

The opposite problem of seeming like we don't want to help is doing someone else's work for them without consent, known as stepping on someone's toes. We may be implying some things about our victim: that they are incompetent, too stupid to succeed at it, or lazy, we don't trust them, or we are better than them. We are also violating an agreement about who is doing what, which can make them not trust *us*. They may suspect us of attitude or being passive aggressive, and resentment is likely to follow. We should never do the work of other people for them unless they have specified that they are okay with this.

This differs from reviewing someone's work, a standard practice in many positions. It is expected, and this is a crucial difference. Agreement makes it cooperation and teamwork. Doing their work for them without permission is the antithesis of both. Claiming we are just being helpful actually makes it more troublesome because we are not acknowledging the wrong we have done or the feelings it has caused. Minimizing the impact of our destructive behavior when it is brought to our attention maximizes its destructiveness.

Redoing someone's work is no better, especially if it isn't our job to do so. Typically, reviewing something means commenting on it and allowing the creator to adjust it, not us doing so for them, but it depends on the work in question. For documentation, edits are often done with a feature like Microsoft Word's "track changes" on; it allows others to see our *suggestions*. So on one hand we have done the edit, but by using this feature, we let others decide whether to accept the improvement. If we did it without track changes on so that they do not know what we've done to it, then we veer into stepping on their toes.

If someone does this and we feel we should say something, we should politely let them know. They may not realize it and it is best to give them the benefit of the doubt, at least the first time. If they are a repeat offender, we may want to schedule a sit down meeting with them to remind them not to do it and explain that it is interfering with our work place satisfaction. Be prepared to cite specific examples and why it is a problem. If the behavior continues beyond this, it might be time to politely involve a manager.

When doing so, it can be wise to avoid naming names at first, especially if we sense that the person we're talking about is more favored than us. We want to avoid showing any attitude about this but be clear that someone else doing–or redoing–our work has called into question our role. We should be open about being concerned and unhappy about this because it can truly lead to ruining our job. Our manager should care about how we feel and be understanding, and if they are not, this is not a good sign about whether they "have our back," a valuable discovery.

Anecdote Time

Early in my career, I worked with a software developer as equals on a project. We had late afternoon meetings, agreeing on who was doing what. With my schedule earlier than hers, I left sooner, and in the morning, I would arrive to discover she had done my work for me. Even if I had wanted to, I could not do the same to her because I didn't know the other technology we were using, and she did. This left me with nothing to do. In response to my question about why she had done this, she laughed it off, and said she started thinking about it, ran with it, and stayed late to finish because she was having fun. I asked her not to do that, but she continued. We argued about it, her laughing it off and saying I was being silly. Then she threw me under the bus to our manager, complaining that she was doing all the work! When I told him what she was doing, he told me to grow up (not the most supportive manager). I was not the only one she did this to, and between others objecting to it and my persistence with our manager, the issue resolved for many of us. However, the woman doing this now had a bad reputation and no one wanted to work with her.

Late in my career, I worked as a consultant and was the only software developer on a small project that was on schedule; my client was a small company. One day, the #2 guy, who was also a programmer, was supposed to move my database code from one platform to another. On Monday, he announced with a smile: "I blew up your database design." This means he had completely restructured it, deleted all of my test data, and made the entire application break. He had fixed part of the app but handed back my mangled software, telling me to fix the rest of what he had broken. His justification? He wouldn't have done it the way I did. When I informed the company owner of this, he said he understood that this was inappropriate, reassured me that they wanted me on the project, and agreed with my suggestion – that the #2 guy at least finish fixing what he'd broken. I did my best not to show that I had lost respect for the perpetrator.

Taking Credit for Someone Else's Work

Among the more unpleasant experiences is when someone takes credit for another's work or ideas. It's unethical, not a good idea, and not something we should do to others. If done to us, it is best to speak up immediately and set the record straight, but to do so as if the one taking credit misspoke or forgot our contribution. Do not do this resentfully (that is attitude, however warranted), even though that is an appropriate reaction. Give the benefit of the doubt no matter how much you suspect it was on purpose. And sometimes it is.

People can also take credit for our work behind our back, which makes it impossible to stop before it is too late to correct. Once something is accepted fact, it is hard to change minds, especially without proof. It's possible that no one will believe us even if we say something, and they may see us as a troublemaker for wanting credit. We can be told that it doesn't matter who achieved something, even when the offender is being rewarded with praise that may positively affect their performance review instead of ours. There are good reasons this stunt produces significant outrage.

Sometimes credit is taken right in front of us in a meeting. This can be so startling and unforeseen that we are mute with disbelief and cannot respond quickly enough. Or calmly enough. The perpetrator may also put up a wall of words we struggle to find a break in. Praise from others can also be heaped on them at once, increasing the feeling of this running away from us too fast to stop it.

The best way to avoid becoming a victim of this is to make sure other people know what we are working on at all times. Then such a lie falls flat. Someone else may even speak up and say they thought we were the achiever, giving us an opportunity to chime in. Ensure it is not just your manager who knows, because they can be the one taking credit. Make sure peers know what you are working on.

Anecdote Time

One job had me writing significant documentation, each of the manuscripts dozens of pages. On the "author" line, I naturally put my name. My manager requested digital copies for his review, and when he sent them back, I saw that, to my astonishment, he had replaced my name with his when making changes. I made more alterations of my own, including putting my name back, and sent the docs to him again. He once again replaced my name and returned them, and I once again replaced his and returned them. I didn't see the documents again, but the programmers and project managers knew I had written them, so when they began circulating with his name on them, everyone knew what he had done and he lost the confidence of his staff. We sometimes have little recourse in such situations, but ensuring everyone knows what we're working on is an innocent way to protect our reputation; taking credit for another's work is a quick way to ruin it.

Email Etiquette

I could probably write an entire book about what goes wrong via email, so I'll only cover some frequent mistakes that are less obvious and yet rampant.

One positive thing we can do is apply the concept of mirroring to email. This means we imitate what someone else is doing to bond with them, not to poke fun. For example, if I sit cross-legged, you sit cross-legged. If they start off by saying "Hello Michael," we respond with "Hello" and their name. If they don't make any sort of greeting and just get right to it, we can skip that, too. If they write Mr. Smith, we might also respond that way. As a side note, it's very rare for people to address someone that way at a job. Everyone is on a first name basis. Being formal like that can be off-putting.

Before emailing, check it for typos and missing words. Others can notice if we often send emails full of mistakes, which suggests we're sloppy or don't care; neither is something we want a reputation for; a manager once criticized me for an unusual number of errors (my sloppiness surprised me), when he cited it as proof I didn't care about my job.

Let's look at other email issues.

Email Format

We might think there is little to email format, and if we go with the defaults established by our job, we would be right. Unfortunately, some people are intent on customizing emails in ways that attract negative attention. Changing the background color away from white is one such mistake. A patterned background is especially bad. It looks unprofessional. We should save that for our personal life. Using fancy fonts or bright colors is similar. Black text on white. That's it. And use a font that no one notices, not something really fancy.

When replying, avoid changing the subject in the email header. In Microsoft Outlook and other modern programs, we can group emails into "conversations" by subject. If we keep altering the subject line, it stops working for everyone who is using that feature. This can be a problem if there are 20 emails that could have been one "conversation" but are now four talks of five emails each. Someone looking for a specific email has to check multiple conversations to find it.

Most of us are familiar with the email signature: one or more lines inserted into our email's ending by the email program. Once we create one, it can be added automatically or manually, and to either replies or only new emails. We usually want our full name, title, phone, and either the division or company for which we work; this is especially helpful if emailing clients. The email address is unnecessary. Keep it brief. This is not an opportunity to show personality. Some clients, government agencies, or employers will dictate our signature contents. If not, we can invent one or borrow someone else's style. An example:

John Doe
Software Architect
Doe Enterprises
555-555-5555 (c)

Read Receipts

While not every job uses Microsoft Outlook, its use is widespread. It includes a feature known as "read receipts." This means we can check an option to turn this on, then send an email. When the recipient clicks on it, Outlook sends us an email, a "read receipt," telling us so. But there's a catch: the first time that user receives such a message, Outlook may prompt them with a message indicating a read receipt has been requested. They can allow or deny it that one time or forever.

Read receipts should never be used, and we should deny them for all people. They imply, "I know you read my email, and I have proof. I know *when* you read it, so you've had all this time and did nothing in response. You may need to defend this." This is passive aggressive, judgmental, and an implied threat. We often focus on our intentions and not enough on the resulting action and how others may interpret it, but we cannot control what others think. Negative reactions to this are commonplace. Read receipts are almost universally reviled.

If we want to know if someone read our email, we follow-up manually in person, via a call, a text, or with another email, in that order of preference. The reason is the ease with which we can manage their interpretation of our follow-up decreases with each of the options in this list. The act of inquiring already implies we expected a response we didn't get, and we are therefore not happy. This disapproval is inherently negative, so we must mitigate this vibe from us. In person, we can view how they are reacting to the follow-up and use body language and voice tone to smooth it over. On the phone, we only have their voice and ours. Texting has none of these but is informal in tone, with copious emojis to soften the blow. And email is the worst and is notorious for others reading tone into our text.

CCing a Manager

We are sometimes emailing with a coworker when one of us adds a manager to the CC line. Everyone can see that the supervisor is now observing the conversation. This can be innocent or passive aggressive. It depends on context, and we should avoid even the appearance of the latter.

It is fine if we need to reply and ask the manager about something that arose during the exchange. But many times, people do not address the added supervisor. We are CCing them so they are aware of what has arisen. This can still be okay, but informing a higher authority often suggests a dispute is arising and they need to step in. This may be necessary and if so, can ruffle feathers. The more contentious the email exchange, the worse this impression is, so this is one way to assess whether CCing our boss is wise.

If we are having a genuine argument, do not CC a manager. Instead, forward it to them and take the high road in what you write. Something like, "He's being a jerk" is not only unprofessional, but shows that we have an attitude, another mistake. We might get ourselves in trouble with the boss or HR. And be aware that someone can always forward our emails to others—including the person we said that about.

An alternative would be to forward the email to the manager with an "FYI" (and no other comments) and then talk to them about it in person. Maybe we only need guidance on how to respond. Or maybe we are tattling on someone, in which case it is smoother to not let that person know. We should be justified in doing this, such as learning the other person will delay our project and our manager needs to know it. In such a case, adding a note such as, "I'm CCing my supervisor just so he is aware" can spare some hard feelings. Don't leave it to chance that they interpret the CC as tattling. Tell them you're not this way. It is up to us to manage how others view our actions.

Reply All

Sometimes people will send a mass email at work. We can reply if we wish, but it is a mistake to use Reply All if our message is intended for less than "all." An example would be responding, "Thanks!" to everyone. No one else needs to see that. While minor, if we consistently do this, we will irritate our coworkers, especially if we and another person start a conversation that has nothing to do with the original message and keep replying all.

The opposite problem can happen—failing to hit Reply All when the message should go to everyone. The lone recipient may realize we did this and have to add everyone back, or we do. When others realize we omitted them, they may wonder if we were trying to cut them out on purpose. They usually see this as an innocent mistake, but it's really easy to give ourselves a reputation for it. It suggests we are careless, thoughtless, or both, and can be one reason people dislike working with us.

Pay attention to the use of Reply All.

Length

Back in the 1990s when the internet was new, pundits predicted the return of the Golden Age of letter writing thanks to email. Nostradamus they were not. Long emails, also known as "novels," are just as frowned upon in the corporate world as anywhere else. If we have that much to say, speak it; it becomes a conversation, which is usually welcome. With email, strive for being succinct without being blunt; too much brevity is one way we can offend and be judged poorly.

Longer emails are less likely to get a response because they are less likely to be read all the way, and people know they might miss something (and look stupid) if they don't read it all first. For example, if our third paragraph talks about the need for something, and they don't read that far and respond that we haven't thought about the need for that thing, it becomes clear they didn't read it. This is embarrassing. We should avoid this mistake ourselves. If we write a long email, we may be "killing them with details." The recipient can shut down and just not deal with a complicated and long email.

The number of issues raised in our email will also directly affect the likelihood of a response, so if we want or need one, be organized. If we would like a response to each question, use a list, but always go with numbers instead of bullets. That way, responders can refer to the issue by number: "For #2, I think..." Bullets are more cumbersome to respond to. I have sometimes reformatted someone's bullets as numbers and then remarked, "I redid the list as numbers so I can refer to them." And then continued. Try to respond to each issue raised so that it doesn't look like we ignored one; this can bother people, especially if they must ask again.

Tone

Controlling email tone is among the hardest feats in the history of humanity. People can read tone into what we've written, and their emotional state affects their interpretation. And we don't know what state they're in when we send or they receive. What might have been okay at one moment is wrong at another. Even worse is that our emotion can subtly affect our writing so that people pickup on *our* emotion as we wrote it. The result is that we can write something that is technically fine but which conveys attitude. And our mood may have nothing to do with them, but it doesn't matter. They can assume it does.

There are countless ways this can happen, but one example is that even the lack of contractions can suggest attitude. Writing "I think we can't achieve this" sounds more casual than "I think we cannot achieve this." Removing "I think" worsens the effect because that is known as hedging and without it, we sound more aggressive. "We cannot achieve that" is much stronger than "I think we can't achieve that." It also sounds inflexible.

At all times, we need to sound cooperative, willing to compromise, and positive. If we have received a message that threatens our own work, such as someone missing a deadline that will cause us to miss ours, writing "is there anything I can do to help?" is light years better than, "You are late! This project will fail because of you." That's extreme, but there are much subtler versions of being judgmental, blaming, and eager to find fault.

If we have an attitude, we have three options: lose it, hide it, or don't interact at all while we've still got it. The first two are very difficult. And we rarely have time to lose it or keep it to ourselves. For most of us, we tend toward being polite in person or even on the phone, so this is the time to interact this way rather than via email. These options also have a powerful advantage: there is no written record of what we said or our tone. And no one can forward it to someone. If anything contentious has arisen at work, or you are in a foul mood (even for reasons that have nothing to do with your job), communicate with your voice. We can certainly reveal an attitude that way as well, but we can see the damage we're doing to ourselves and instantly correct it ("Sorry, I'm just frustrated with my own work") before it's too late.

Inappropriate Jokes

Joking at work is a great way to reduce tension and bond with others. For some people, it is their primary way of relating. But not all jokes are created equal. We should obviously steer clear of sexualized ones or similarly inappropriate subjects, but there is another risk—people making jokes at our expense. None of us like this, so do not do this to others.

There's a version of this that is worse–jokes that paint us as poorly doing our job or which blame us for something that went wrong. The problem here is being cast in a negative light. This isn't a minor nuisance; it is possible that the wheels are being greased for the same sentiment being said in the future without a trace of joking. And this can be so serious that it costs us our job.

Don't laugh good-naturedly if it happens, as this condones it and invites a repeat. Instead, adopt a more serious expression and choose your words carefully. We can calmly say we don't find being mocked or blamed funny, even though they meant it as a joke (give them the benefit of the doubt that no harm was meant). Using a word like "mocked" can sober many people because it suggests bullying and a hostile work environment, two areas that HR takes seriously and where legal consequences may exist. We should be careful not to go too far with our disapproval, as this can cause a backlash that helps no one. Going to HR over it, or threatening to, is risky and may get us labeled as a troublemaker.

If we can't sober up the perpetrator with our response, they are unlikely to apologize. Often, the people who make such jokes in the first place won't apologize, and will instead insist they were just joking, that we need to lighten up, that we are so serious, and that we have no sense of humor. Each of these responses is known as "minimizing" our interpretation and therefore us. The goal is to exonerate themselves and further cast us as the problem. This is manipulative and passive aggressive. It also means we should stop joking with this person from now on. If people conclude we can't take a joke about this, *that is what we want* because it will inhibit them from doing it further—at least to our face.

Avoiding this ahead of time is the best approach, and we do this by not establishing too much of a casual, anything goes joking style with another coworker. It can be pleasant to feel like we are friends instead of coworkers, but this way lies trouble. Always remember that this is our job, and it is more important than companionship. Once people have normalized criticizing us, we can become a scapegoat when something serious happens. This often requires other things to go wrong at work, but it happens, and not everything is in our control. Not tolerating casual contempt absolutely is.

Anecdote Time

In one position I held, a Vice President had an assistant who was fresh out of college and often joked with me. One day the assistant jokingly asked me why I was repeatedly missing a mandatory meeting every day—a *month* after it had started. I jokingly responded that my attendance obviously wasn't required if she had never told me about it. She forwarded it to management, and they hauled me into a meeting and lectured me on my "attitude." While I was able to clear up what was really happening, I never joked with the assistant again.

Hallway Meetings

There are two acceptable places to hold a meeting: in a room or at someone's desk (usually when only 2-3 people are involved). But a third option often arises—the hallway. People do not do this on purpose, but it happens when two or more people in said corridor encounter each other. And then they have an impromptu conversation that turns into a meeting, which is any conversation that lasts longer than five minutes. That is the point at which one participant should realize it has become a conference and suggest they take it elsewhere. Why?

Because hallways are not designed for this, but for getting around. By being stationary in a hallway for an extended time, we inhibit its intended purpose. It can bother people, depending on how many people are in this impromptu meeting, how loud it is, and how much maneuvering others must do to get around the obstacle thus created. The strength of the irritation increases with the duration of the conversation.

And one major reason is that hallways are often next to a cube farm or offices, not away from everyone's desk. This means twenty or more people must hear a distracting conversation about subjects not involving them. It doesn't much matter if these subjects are personal or not. Hallway meetings are an act of thoughtlessness. We should avoid them and suggest to other participants to take it elsewhere.

But what do we do when we are not a participant? It is difficult to interrupt and ask people to talk elsewhere in a way that is not off-putting. Many of us sense this and keep quiet, which worsens our displeasure. We can feel that the talkers are being rude, but if we say something, they will consider us rude. It is easy to show attitude while doing it, and that's another mistake we must avoid.

The trick to asking is to apologize for interrupting and then casually and politely ask if they wouldn't mind moving the conversation. We can remark about difficulty concentrating, for example, but just try not to seem judgmental about their activity.

Clothing

There are three styles of attire expected at work, depending on our role and the occasion: formal, business casual, and casual. For men, formal is clearly the suit and tie, but even a blazer qualifies. Women have similar more reserved outfits that can be worn, such as a business suit. Unless we are an executive, in which case we probably are not reading this book, we are often in business casual dress. When in doubt what constitutes this, we ask HR and they will be glad we sought confirmation. They usually reserve casual attire for casual days or events like a company picnic.

While it is obvious to not wear shirts with vulgar slogans, and companies often have policies forbidding sensitive subjects (like politics), there are other gaffes we can make. Showing too much skin is one. This includes low-cut blouses that may not offer a view of cleavage... until you bend over, which can happen for many reasons, such as plugging a monitor into the back of a laptop while at a meeting table. For men, we have the infamous plumber's crack. Both genders can wear clothes that reveal a tattoo, and these are often considered risqué even if they aren't. Remember that as the day goes on, we could find ourselves in a position we were not expecting when we got dressed, such as crawling under a desk to plug in something. A female HR Manager once summed up suitable attire by saying, "If you can see up it, down it or through it, don't wear it, and that goes for men and women alike."

Office buildings are notorious for temperature control, meaning we have none. We are at someone else's mercy. We will quickly learn if the environment tends toward cold, warm, or the rare just right. But AC and heater fails happen. It is wise to keep a light jacket or sweater at our desk or at least in our car. Even a change of shirt can be wise. I have worked in places so cold that I wore long johns in the winter, and places that grew so hot because of an AC failure that I removed an undershirt and rolled sleeves up as far as I could.

When starting a job, it is wise to begin conservative and reconnoiter to see how others are dressed. Fitting in is important because people make assumptions based on our clothes. And assumptions about us are seldom favorable. Being too formal can be just as bad as being too casual. Ask HR before the first day and confirm that business casual is expected, unless our role dictates otherwise. We can also ask our manager.

LinkedIn

Not having a LinkedIn account, which is free, is a mistake because it provides an important benefit: being able to track down former coworkers and managers. If we want to network or ask for a reference after having already left a company, we might only have their work information. What if they also left? Now we can't reach them. LinkedIn solves this dilemma.

It doesn't matter much when we reach out to them, with one exception. Doing it within the first month or two of working with people can seem overeager. This is a minor concern, but people are more likely to accept if they have known us longer. There is no rush.

LinkedIn also provides the option of seeing their work history and later, where and when they've moved on. This can be useful if they have landed somewhere enviable and become an admired person in our network. Someone may reach out to us for a reference, asking if we know of a position, or suggesting they've got one for us. We don't need to spend significant amounts of time on the site, either, and many people largely ignore it once set up. The small time investment can pay off handsomely.

It is also worth noting that LinkedIn is primarily for professional use and should be treated as such. Our personal approach to social media is best left on platforms like Facebook. Politics in particular is something to avoid in many areas, but the divisiveness of this can impact us more if we engage in it on LinkedIn. Many successful professionals never make a comment, post an article, or do anything more than keep their profile up to date and, even after a decade on the site, have less than 500 connections, so we don't need to attempt garnering attention with many posts and comments. Let them come naturally.

CHAPTER TWO

The Workday

The time we spend at work is where everything good, bad, and in between happens.

Work Hours

For full-time staff, an eight-hour workday is usually the default. Five in a row, Monday through Friday, meets our requirement for 40 hours per week.

Flexible Schedules

Some companies allow for flexible schedules. This can mean several options exist.

Management might allow us to work nine-hour days and then take every other Friday off. Or work ten-hour days and take one day off every week. Or if we need to leave 1-2 hours early one day, we might be allowed to make up those missed hours another day within the pay period (instead of using vacation hours). This means that if the period is from the 1st to the 15th of the month, and we are going to leave early on the 15th, we cannot make up the hours after this. But if we know it is going to happen, we can get permission to compensate ahead of that, such as on the 14th.

The willingness to allow this varies from company to company, manager to manager, and client to client. If this flexibility is important to us, it is best to ask about it during the recruitment phase. Companies will sometimes get it wrong, and the policy can also change without warning. We have little to no recourse when this happens.

Anecdote Time

One manager of mine did not like any variation to a routine. If I worked 7 AM–3 PM, he wanted no changes. I could miss time and use vacation to cover it, but he disapproved of leaving early one day and making it up the next, though he never denied a request. Even some dates being for my difficult divorce, which he knew about, got me the dirty look that made me feel like I was in trouble. I stopped asking, and because of the volume of such needs that year, I could not go on vacation; I had used all of my hours. One way to handle this is to directly ask our manager what their preference is. We are hoping for a goof work-life balance, but we may need to accept that this particular person doesn't agree with our take on that.

Core Hours

Many jobs have core working hours. This typically means that while start and finish times may vary, we must be at work from either 9 or 10 AM until 2 or 3 PM. It varies by the job. If the core hours go until 3 PM, we can work 7 to 3 PM, but not 6-2 PM. Or at least, not normally. Managers are sometimes flexible about this. Core hours does not usually mean we can't make an appointment during those hours (check with your employer). It means that our normal schedule must include *all* of the core hours.

Be aware that a project or team may have important/required meetings or events outside core hours, though this is usually after 3 PM. This means we would miss it, and this might not be allowed. Learn what the required calendar events are before deciding on a schedule and plan accordingly. It is best to ask whether our intended hours are okay during the hiring phase, but of course we may be employed there far beyond the original plan. Once we have established our schedule and that we are a valued staff member, we may get some consideration regarding a conflict, meaning someone agrees to move the meeting, or we can call in while driving home, for example.

Being Late

The corporate world is not usually one where we punch-in an exact time and leave at one either, but this depends on our country, and we are still expected to be on time. Being 5-10 minutes late can be a non-issue provided we make it up by staying late the same day, and it is wise to be visible doing so, and tell our manager. Transparency is important. Most understand that life happens. Even then, we do not want to make a habit of it. Another option is being early often, but then still staying until our usual exit time anyway, meaning we have routinely put in a few extra minutes and get a free pass when slightly late instead. Some managers are sticklers for punctuality, and we need to assess the attitude of ours by learning their reaction when we speak to them about it.

All of this differs from being over fifteen minutes late. We should call, send a text, or fire off an email with an estimate of when we'll be there. A heads up is appreciated and prevents managers from thinking we are unaware of our lateness, don't care, or are screwing around. Maybe we can't be trusted. Or maybe something happened to us. If we get a message from them asking where we are, this is bad and they will watch us more in the future. Don't make them do this. Be proactive and contact them first.

Their manager or someone else may look for us, and if we're that late, it looks bad for our manager to admit they don't know where we are if asked. This seems like they don't have good authority over us. Expect that authority to increase. The flexibility we once enjoyed may vanish. If we arrive before our manager, this changes nothing. Other managers or coworkers can notice and tell them.

Meetings

Meetings have an unfortunate tendency to be boring to many people, which is one reason many dislike them. It may also cause mistakes we can make while attending.

And the first is being late. This is especially bad if managers are there, but our peers may dislike it as well. It depends on the culture at the job because this varies widely. On some teams, everyone is five minutes early. At others, people roll in and out at random. Don't let tardy colleagues influence you. Be on time. We all have smartphones and can spend the time waiting doing something. This looks better than coming late.

Don't bring food (or at least, don't eat it) to a meeting unless invited to, or it is for everyone (and you have permission for that). A manager might get away with it, but it is rude and distracting. It can also leave a mess. There is a good chance of needing to speak when there is food in our mouth; doing it is bad, but so is everyone having to wait and watch us chew. Both bring attention to what we are doing.

Bringing our work laptop is required if we are presenting from it, but it can otherwise be a negative if we appear to be working instead of listening. Appearances matter. Taking notes on it is great, but if we are mostly using our mouse, people know we're doing something else. It can seem like we are multi-tasking, with the implication that we are a hard worker, but we have limited control over how other people interpret what we're doing—i.e., not listening. If others see our screen's notes, that is ideal. If they see us choosing our fantasy football team, not so much.

Smartphones are another issue. They should be muted, but we must also not appear to do more than glance at it, or maybe jot off a quick message or read one. Staring at it suggests we are playing a game, reading a book, or otherwise not paying attention. We should not take a call during a meeting unless it is important or we have permission, and we should excuse ourselves to leave the room for its duration. In some cultures, even a glance at the phone is considered rude, so know your locale.

We can call in to some meetings rather than attend in person. This is obvious if we are physically elsewhere, but sometimes we are nearby and call in anyway. Find out from management if this is okay before doing it, even if you see others doing this. This is the best way to multi-task while attending a meeting, whether or not it is work-related. Don't forget to mute yourself and be quick to unmute and respond if called upon. One problem here is being out of sight, out of mind; it is wise to be seen.

Anecdote Time

While at NASA, I worked with a junior colleague who was routinely late to his own meetings by over ten minutes. To make matters worse, we had to leave our building and either walk or even drive to another building to attend, because of closer rooms being booked. Some buildings being quite large also meant it took considerable time to find the room. To be on time meant a fifteen-minute commute. This meant leaving my desk at 10:45 for the 11 AM meeting, waiting until 11:15 with him as a no-show, and finally leaving to return by 11:30, at which point he once emailed asking if I was coming because he had finally arrived. He seemed to think this was fine despite multiple people telling him otherwise. His coworkers did not respect his handling of these avoidable moments, partly because he didn't listen. Try to hear the feedback coworkers provide. It is valuable.

Food at Work

Food is part of corporate life. At the least, we need to eat lunch, whether we leave to do it or not. There are several issues that arise.

One is that food often leaves a mess. We must clean this up regardless of where it happens: at our desk, in the microwave, a counter, or the floor. We should be more fastidious than we are even at home. Making a mess is fine; leaving one is not. With repetition, people will know it's us. Even if we think no one is in the kitchen with us and we can sneak out and leave the mess behind, someone might walk in at that moment. Leaving a mess for someone else to clean up shows a lack of respect. Rising above that takes only a few moments of work.

Storing Food

When not eating food, we must store it somewhere.

If one exists, the refrigerator is the obvious place for some items. Most offices have one, but sometimes it is so crowded that we will never get to use it. Always put your name on anything that goes in: leftovers, drinks, salad dressing, and more. Someone may have a similar container or leftovers from the same restaurant. Our food is likely to be moved to make space so someone can add or remove their own. Expect this and don't get offended; we do not own the spot where we placed our item. Food gets stolen from the refrigerator. It is uncommon, and we should never do this, but if we suspect ours is gone, we should look thoroughly rather than jump to conclusions and make accusations. The only way to avoid being a victim is to not use the fridge.

Coworkers may have a fridge cleaning schedule that is posted on it, sometimes with the name of the cleaner; it often rotates among peers who are seldom thanked for the service, and saying something to them is a simple way to make someone feel appreciated. On the scheduled days (usually a Friday), everything inside the fridge is thrown in the trash and the appliance is cleaned. They may send an email reminder of this impending apocalypse, but don't count on it. Pay attention to the sign on the fridge door and be proactive about cooperating. And don't show resentment if your food gets tossed—avoiding this was *your* job.

If we don't want to use the fridge and our food still needs to keep cool until lunch, one option is the insulated lunch box. Even without an ice pack, these can keep food cool enough to not spoil for four hours or more (the contents may just be reaching room temperature). These avoid the problems with the fridge, so if we find the latter causing us to get an attitude, we should try this solution. Unless we buy lunch, we need to bring it in to work and these containers are designed for easy carrying. We can also store utensils in them, needing nothing from work.

We may also want to store snacks at our desk. The best option is a sealable container so that vermin cannot get to them overnight. Never leave food exposed, even if intending to put it in the trash the next day. Trash is often cleaned out overnight by cleaning crews (partly because of food in trash bins), but this varies by the workplace. Do yourself and others a favor and avoid leaving anything that attracts pests.

The Microwave

A microwave is often available and has several etiquette requirements.

One is to clean any mess made inside it. Appropriately cover food while heating it to avoid messes. But if it happens, just take care of it. Or the next person to use it will discover it and be none too pleased. That next person may be us. This is a "do unto others as you would have them do unto you" moment. No one cares we made a mess (they assume it to be an accident), only that we didn't take care of it. If we're seen cleaning anything (this included), we build a reputation of being a good office mate. Good things happen to those who clean.

Many people start the microwave and then walk away. This is fine if we are back before it is done. But no one enjoys opening the microwave to discover someone else's food is still in there—and there's no sign of them. Are we to wait? To remove their item so we can start ours? Many are unsure of the etiquette here. It's customary to wait 30-60 seconds to see if that person will arrive. After that, etiquette now dictates we don't have to wait anymore and can remove their food to the counter and use the microwave ourselves. To avoid being this person, pay attention, set a timer on your smartphone, or don't leave. It is rude to not be back in time and we should apologize if busted. Some people think we are in the wrong to remove their dish, especially if they need to restart it, but they are wrong.

All of this applies to using the office toaster, too, if available. The difference there is that people would have to touch our food to remove it, and they won't. This makes our absence especially irritating. Plates are often not available for this, meaning we'll be using a paper towel.

The Coffee Machine

If we use a coffee or tea dispenser at work, etiquette requires us to clean up spills of liquid or sugar, etc., and put any wrappers in the trash. We should also learn to fill it for the inevitable moment when we drink the last of it. We should treat these appliances like we are at home, we own them, and we are being a good host for guests (or coworkers). This includes noting that supplies have run out and informing the office manager responsible for replacing them.

Where to Eat

Some workplaces have a cafeteria or kitchen in which we can eat, but many don't. This typically means eating at our desk, a practice so commonplace that no one finds it odd. There may be picnic tables outside, but don't count on it. If we don't have a desk but a shared table, this means eating in front of others. Given that we have no other option, this is acceptable. Eating lunch before 11 may cause a raised eyebrow, some people not understanding that we may have eaten breakfast at 5:30 to start by 6:30 or 7 AM. If eating after 1 PM causes a reaction, it doesn't have a negative connotation, usually. It seems to imply that we were working so hard we didn't have a chance to eat.

If we walk up to someone's office or cubicle and discover that they're eating lunch, we should excuse ourselves and offer to come back later, unless we expect to take under a minute of their time. But these conversations can often get carried away and now their food is going cold. Try to avoid this. They'll say and act like they don't mind, but many people do and just aren't telling us out of politeness—and hoping we know they're lying and will go away for 5-10 minutes so they can finish.

If our victim (er, I mean coworker) is only snacking on something, none of this applies. Why? Because they could snack for the next two hours for all we know. Snacks aren't consumed all at once like an actual meal, which is typically shorter. Circling back in a few minutes is one thing, but having to repeatedly come around because they're still munching is ridiculous. Typically, a snacking coworker expects to be interrupted while food is sticking out of their mouth.

Be aware that some organizations have rules about not having open drink containers at our desk because we might spill liquid on equipment that is subsequently damaged or even destroyed. This needs to be respected. The solution is a sealable container and a good habit of always closing it tight even between sips. Knocking it over by accident is far less of an issue when nothing can emerge from it.

Forbidden Foods

Some people are very sensitive to smells. The result is that they may forbid some items at work. This is an unspoken policy or there are signs near the microwave; it usually isn't serious enough to be in the employee handbook. For every person who thinks the smell is wonderful, there's another that hates it; we cannot assume otherwise.

Two common foods are popcorn and cooked fish. Both have a powerful scent when heated in a microwave. The smell lasts quite a while and spreads well. Eating these at work is not the issue so much as cooking or warming them. We may need to prepare them at home and eat them cold. Use common sense or ask someone. The consideration is appreciated.

The Meals

It is expected that we'll eat lunch during work hours, but dinner is uncommon. Breakfast does sometimes happen because some will arrive and eat it within the first hour. Otherwise, there is no actual difference between them for etiquette.

Some offices have bagel day. Despite its name, there may be fruits, croissants, and pastries as well. Usually spreads and yogurt abound, but it varies by the office.

These are provided free by the employer and we should at least occasionally be seen partaking; otherwise, it seems like we are refusing hospitality, not that anyone is taking notes. But who doesn't like free food?

One issue here is to not be a pig and take too much, unless we are circling back later for leftovers. Sometimes this is actually appreciated because it reduces waste or those in charge of this from figuring out what to do with it. Similarly, employers sometimes supply food at other intervals or occasions. One is pizza day, or to welcome a new employee. At the least, occasionally put in an appearance.

Some countries have laws that require us to take a thirty minute break for every five or more hours that we work. Circumnavigating this can be illegal, and if we have a workplace accident or repetitive stress injury, and it can be proven we were skipping these breaks, we could lose something like worker's compensation. Our employer should tell us of such regulations. In many workplaces, posters are in the kitchen or break area for such things, and while there is a tendency to look right past these, pay attention to them. There is a reason these are there instead of kitten and puppy pictures, and one reason is liability – the employer has effectively told us.

If we leave for lunch, remember that this is not work time aside from possibly being a required break. We must make up all of it. We don't need permission to leave because we are adults, but it never hurts to admit to a manager that we're running out for lunch. If we take twenty minutes to get it and bring it back, stay twenty minutes later at work. The math is simple.

We can also eat at our desk and work at the same time. We get a free pass on this. For those who are time conscious and don't want to stay longer than eight hours of work time, this is a way to not stay extra. But some contracts, employers, or clients can state that we must take thirty minutes for lunch. This can be frustrating if we are prone to bringing it in and scarfing it down, because we end up with nothing to do for the remaining time unless we are working... an extra twenty-five minutes? It may be something to discuss with our manager, that we don't really take the break. Some will be sticklers for the rules, while others will wave it off. Assess your manager's attitude by asking. A question is always more appreciated than an assumption.

Office Leftovers and Snacks

There are sometimes events involving food. Whether or not we were invited or attended, leftovers can exist. Afterward, these are often placed in a location where all office staff can help themselves. This will usually be the kitchen area, or at least where the microwave and refrigerator are. Rarely is there a sign indicating we can partake of the food, so we may need to ask other staff who are more familiar with what happens. The answer is typically yes, help yourself. The food has served its purpose and will go to waste.

We can build some good will by occasionally bringing snacks for coworkers. But we don't put a big sign next to it saying that they are courtesy of us. It can look manipulative, like we did it for praise, not for anyone's enjoyment. If we want people to know, we time our placing of the snack to when the location has witnesses. Or we walk through an area with people there. If someone comments on our generosity, it can also be good to downplay it, such as saying, "Well, it was my turn," because others have done something similar (assuming they have) and we've been gobbling up those snacks. This makes us seem like a team player, too. All we need is one person to know. When others ask who brought it in, they'll answer for us.

Sometimes a coworker will have snacks available for everyone. Even if we don't particularly like anything, we should sometimes take something to accept rather than reject their hospitality. If the person providing these ever says that donations are appreciated, immediately make that donation. Otherwise, we might feel guilty about taking part in this without an opportunity to contribute. This can be one reason to bring something in.

Anecdote Time

I once worked for a company as one of three consultants. Official corporate policy dictated that we could not receive any corporate benefits. We were to be excluded from the monthly pizza day and the weekly bagel event, but we joined in anyway, under the radar and with manager approval. They would remind us we were technically not allowed, but they thought the policy was going too far. Sometimes, the company did a more official event with a raffle after the food. We were always told to leave. In our minds, they considered us second-class citizens. In such a situation, we must handle it with grace.

Bathroom Habits

What happens in the bathroom stays in the bathroom is mostly true, but not always. People will notice some habits, the biggest being whether we wash our hands after relieving ourselves. We must avoid even the appearance of not doing this; I once worked somewhere with auto-flush urinals and as I approached the door to leave, it flushed and likely gave the impression to someone entering that I had just peed and was now leaving immediately. The only solution was having a paper towel that I had dried my hands on still in my hand, implying I had just come from the sink. Multiple people may notice and sometimes they will get to talking about it.

We can do ourselves a favor and use the paper towel on which we dried our hands to grab the door handle. This reduces the risk of catching even a cold from others. We can also use it to wipe the handle off for others, a miniature act of public service. With the door already open, we may then toss the towel into a garbage can if one is next to the door, as it often is. If not, carry it until the next trash can is found.

Other habits can be addressed, but most fall under the same idea—treat the bathroom like it is in your home. Don't leave a mess, always flush, and try to prevent anyone from thinking less of you for what you do.

CHAPTER THREE

Our Work Environment

Our environment can have a significant impact on us, particularly when we dislike it. We usually have no choice where we sit, or who is next to us, or anything, really. Feeling concern about this prior to our first day, or when there is an office relocation pending, is normal. But this way lies madness. Given that we have no control, we must usually surrender to fate.

Locations

Great variety exists in our workspace if we are not home. We may get an office, cube, or open table. Each has its concerns.

A Place to Call Our Own?

If we have an office or cube, we usually have a designated seat. This means we can store our belongings there, and it is unlikely that anyone will disturb them even after we are gone for the day. Items go missing from desks, though this is rare. Lock it up if concerned about it, and if something goes missing, report it to your manager. Sometimes the cleaning crew, who are usually outside contractors, has a thief among them.

If we "own" our space, we can decorate it, but don't go overboard. Some people cover every visible wall space with pictures of flowers, friends, or whatever else, and the result is an eyesore. We should also not cover the desk with too much paraphernalia. Less than a half-dozen non-work items on the desk, and another six on the walls, is a fair guideline.

There is a variation of "owning" our space where we share it with someone. The catch is that only one of us is there at a time. This means the other is working from home that day. This comes in various flavors, including two dedicated people alternating with each other. Both "own" the space, but there must be cooperation and trust. It is advised to have an in-person meeting, or at least a video call, where the storage is divided up. This can work well with a respectful partnership, or it can be a nightmare without one.

Another option is called hoteling. This means that there are cubes or workstations, but they are not permanently assigned. We may need to reserve a spot via an app. This is similar to "hot-desking," where seats are taken on a first-come, first-serve basis that can lead to competition for preferred seats, and unnecessary angst. Both have a disadvantage of not "owning" the space, which also means needing to carry everything we need because we may not be able to leave things at work at all. With people being creatures of habit, some dislike this. And it may prevent us from bonding with some coworkers if we seldom sit near them day after day. On the other hand, it can help us get to know more people, albeit it more casually.

No matter the circumstances, we seldom have much control and must accept the workspace we are given. That said, when changes are afoot, it is common for grumbling to occur out of manager earshot, but try to be a listener and not a contributor. Sharing gripes is one way coworkers bond, so don't chastise those who are complaining.

Offices

Offices tend to be reserved for managers, but even they may not get them. Most people seem to prefer one because of privacy. We don't have anyone watching us or our screen. Only our neighbors may overhear our conversations, but we can prevent that by closing the door. We may get away with quietly listening to a radio without earbuds. They often have a window, but not always. The window can be a negative if it causes the room to overheat from the sun, which is more likely given the enclosed space.

Offices cause less impromptu socializing, which may be a pro or con depending on personality. The reason is precisely not overhearing what others are saying and joining in. We must purposely go to where they are for that. We can find offices isolating. Despite these disadvantages, everyone seems to want one. We sometimes share an office with a peer, where each of us has a desk or a cubicle.

If we have an office, we should leave the door open unless needing privacy for a meeting or phone call. People will wonder what we're hiding if we don't. It also seems too antisocial. People aren't sure if they should knock or if we're in, and we don't want to create the impression we are absent if we're present. Unexplained absences, or even the appearance of them, lower the trust with which coworkers view us. Being seen has value.

Cubicles

The cubicle is standard for many parts of the world. They are not all created equal. Taller ones provide better privacy and noise reduction. Shorter ones can have walls so low that they seemingly don't exist, allowing more visual and auditory distractions. Some have walls that are easier to attach papers to, and most come with several drawers for storage.

Then there is cubicle placement. A preferred spot is often one with less traffic, such as by a window, with only one person visible across from us and no one behind. This provides the option of fewer people seeing our screen. The worst cube is usually one at an intersection of hallways, with a meeting room right there, as this causes maximum traffic and potential meetings where people don't close the door and we have to listen to it. But there is something worse...

A Table

Sometimes there are no offices or cubes, and staff sit in a meeting room to work all day on the conference table. This means sitting right next to someone who can see everything we do so that there is no privacy. Those sitting across from us can see every facial expression or every moment of distraction. And every sound someone makes is exceptionally audible, whether it's typing, chewing on lunch or snacks, breathing, or something else. This is among the most distracting of environments. We may sit in a different spot each day, but one is the same as another. We have nowhere to store anything from day-to-day, and must take and bring everything with us. When this is combined with having nowhere to eat lunch except where we work, it worsens. We know our environment is bad when we wish we had a cubicle, which has long been loathed, but some things are better than we know.

Anecdote Time

One job had me sitting elbow-to-elbow with a coworker at a table barely wide enough for us and our laptops. I studiously kept my eyes on my screen, hoping he would do the same. On the plus side, we had a bay window overlooking D.C. streets. Too bad the balcony door wouldn't stay closed, and the winter air poured in. We wore jackets and sometimes our gloves.

Open Floor Plans

Another unpleasant situation for many is the "open floor plan." This means everyone has a desk (though maybe not permanently), but there are no cubes or walls except the four surrounding scores of desks. There is therefore far less privacy. We can be seen by someone as far as fifty feet away. Everyone knows when we leave our desk, where we go, and how long we're gone. We can feel like we're being watched from all sides, not because anyone is actually staring at us, but because people may face us from every direction. We can also see many of our coworkers and find this distracting. If we have a habit like chewing on our lip while thinking, everyone will know. Sound travels far, a known problem that causes some employers to offer noise-canceling headphones, which is a sign they should probably put up some walls.

Anecdote Time

I once did an interview where, when I walked into the lobby, the receptionist waited to my right, and to my left was a floor-to-ceiling glass wall, beyond which were roughly fifty people in an open floor plan. Once I confirmed that was where I would be seated if hired, I bombed the interview on purpose.

At the State Department, a new upper management guy removed all the cubicles for an open floor plan. He repeatedly asked staff what we wanted via surveys and "town halls," and we provided near universal opposition with detailed reasons. He ignored it all and did it anyway. It would not affect *him*, of course—except that everyone loathed him for it. In these scenarios, our best bet is to give it a chance and see what we like about it, and how to mitigate what we don't. For example, there are overlays that can be added to screens to prevent others from watching our every computer move; we may need permission, and our employer may even purchase them. It can't hurt to ask.

At Home

Prior to Covid-19 in 2020, only some of us had the luxury of working from home (WFH). Today, many more of us do, though this is subject to change. WFH has both pros and cons, like everything, and we may be far more familiar with these now.

If we can WFH, we must usually agree to a policy that specifies our responsibilities. This agreement may come from our employer or the agency/client for whom we ultimately work; there may be two, in which case the latter often takes precedence. When in doubt, ask management. Most agreements are straightforward, even common sense, but some are quite rigid and even require photos of a dedicated workspace and proof of workman's compensation insurance. A frequent refrain is to not abuse the privilege, lest we lose it. It is not a right, though it may be required post Covid-19. Abusing it takes the right away and possibly our job.

Jobs will dictate how many days per week we can work from home, and this is usually not negotiable, but if it is, we should ask during the hiring phase. It is okay to say that we cannot take the position without a certain number of WFH days. A difficult commute is an acceptable reason. Most recruiters have a sense of traffic patterns between our home and a job, but not always if the recruiter is not local. We can inform them of this and say we can't consider it without that. This is something people understand. However, even if we agreed on this, WFH often cannot start until some initial period has passed, such as 30-90 days. Find out the options.

If they gave us WFH days less than five per week, we may be able to choose them. Once we do, they expect us to keep them. Occasional changes in circumstances are fine, with manager approval. They may ask us to come in on a WFH day and we must do so without complaint, but we can ask if we can swap it with another. If the answer is no, gracefully accept this. It's always best to pose a request as a question. For example, "Can I work from home on Friday?" is better than, "I'm working from home Friday."

Even before Covid-19, some jobs required us to work from home. A shortage of desks and office space is a major reason, but it also helps corporate expenses via smaller spaces. This can mean that we share a spot with someone at the office, but only one of us is there at a time, as discussed previously in this chapter.

Working from home is not without its issues. Some managers assume we're not working at all and it's therefore in our best interests to prove it. We're unlikely to be openly accused of not working unless it's obvious. What's more likely is an air of suspicion, disapproval, or disrespect that makes us uncomfortable. Just as some assume we don't work while at home, others assume we do if we are present at our workplace. This may have nothing to do with us, and probably does not. These assumptions probably don't reflect out true work patterns, but they can be difficult to turn around. This is not a recommendation, but for appearances, it can actually be better to spend an entire workday in the office and accomplish nothing than to work hard while at home and be assumed to be doing nothing.

One goal is to always have something to show when asked for it. Doing nothing all day and being unexpectedly asked to show our work is not a position we want to be in. Always get assignments done first before any down time. Managers will sometimes ask what we'll be working on; have an answer and then do it. Planning for these moments makes handling them easier.

Try to keep a set schedule while working from home, even if it differs from the office one. We may even want to add that to our email signature. People like knowing what to expect and then having that expectation met. It creates confidence in us. And the set schedule may ward off the temptations at home. It can also allow us to set boundaries, such as not working after we reach close of business for us. Logging out of a work computer also helps this.

Video Calls

Whether Zoom or another technology, many of us are now quite familiar with video calls for work. With common sense, these are easy to accommodate, but some are more challenging than others.

As with in-person or call-in meetings, it is better to be early than late. We should also expect connection issues and log on five minutes prior. It is wise to start muted and leave ourselves that way until we have something to say. This is especially helpful if there is any background noise; with twenty people, it accumulates.

That it is a video call seems to imply that they expect us to be on camera, but this is not true. We may just need to see someone's screen or share ours. Regardless, always be prepared to be on video. Consult with management regarding the attire expected from home, but it is often casual, while avoiding questionable slogans on shirts, for example. Our background should also contain nothing objectionable or distracting to others.

Those who desire a more professional look may want to invest in lighting, the details of which are outside the scope of this book. But there are countless articles about vlogging or making YouTube videos, the focus on affordable lighting and techniques to create an impressive look. We can achieve this for under $100 and that is a small price to pay, especially when we are doing job interviews this way, and every ounce of professionalism helps. Having the space to leave dedicated lighting up all the time is easier than having to set up repeatedly.

Instant Messaging

Many companies have an instant messenger program both installed and activated by default on the work laptop. These often default to something like showing us as "away" when there's no mouse or keyboard activity for 15 minutes. We can change this or sign out, but the latter looks suspicious unless we're never on, even at the office. As for the former, some programs show how long we're idle. "Away 30 minutes" is worse than "Away 15 minutes." Telling people we're stepping away is wise because we planned it and this suggests we are not goofing around—even if we just planned to goof around.

If we're always signed out, we'll know if a manager complains because they'll do so long before our WFH day arrives. They might do it, too. Other managers might be on the lookout for it. Get the "lay of the land" on this. Are coworkers often contacting you through instant message? Or never? In the former case, we need to stay on and use it, too. In the latter, that means no one is really using it, or not with us anyway.

Instead of messenger, some companies will say we have to email them or a distribution group when we log on, off, or take a break. We can sometimes forget (this happens), but we shouldn't do that too often or it looks like a ruse. Some will send this message and then go eat breakfast, for example, so they are not actually working, but that sort of thing happens when we're at work, too, socializing with people and otherwise not doing work. Find your balance and be at peace with it.

There is one advantage to messenger—we can be on longer than our stated hours. Why would we want to do this? For appearances. It looks better to be on for 9 hours when we only need 8 than to be on for 7 hours and 45 minutes. We won't charge the extra time, and we won't be working, but it creates an appearance of definitely getting in our required time.

Anecdote Time

When I worked at State, I worked from home Monday, Wednesday, and Friday for one week and Tuesday and Thursday the next. My manager would randomly call me at home when he had a question, but he'd also first ask, "Are you working today?" I could never tell if he was joking (we had a good relationship), but the question always made me uncomfortable, so I asked him to stop that, using a light-hearted tone to avoid the appearance of attitude. He chuckled but stopped after a few iterations; sometimes we must be patient.

Noise

We can seldom do much to quiet the surrounding noise at work, but we can avoid contributing to it unnecessarily. Loud talkers and other excessively noisy people are often disliked quietly (see what I did there?). We should keep our voice at a reasonable volume and not have conversations with people ten or more feet from us. We should also avoid using a speakerphone because hearing our side of a conversation is bad enough; most coworkers really do not want to hear the other side of it, too. We can often use ear buds for these, eliminating the need. We should also watch any video feed, such as a meeting, this way. If we have a squeaky chair, see about getting it fixed or replaced.

These things can truly irritate us with repetition, and while they won't cost us a job, creating an attitude about us isn't wise. Similarly, we can seldom say anything to others about the noise they are creating because our unhappiness comes across and bothers them. There is value to learning to work with music on in our earbuds, as it can drown out much we dislike.

Anecdote Time

I once had a coworker with a keyboard so loud that everyone could hear it three cubicle rows over. He often apologized for the clacking but wouldn't stop using it because it helped his carpal tunnel syndrome. Most of us were fairly certain similar but quieter keyboards existed, so some were not sympathetic. If we find ourselves apologizing often, this may be a sign to search for alternatives if for no other reason than to assure others that we truly have no other choice.

Building Amenities

Just as jobs and employers are not created equal, neither are the buildings in which we work.

Security

As expected, all buildings have lockable doors, at the least, but beyond this, the security in place varies considerably. We may need a scannable picture badge to get past security doors, guards, or machines—or all three. Before we're badged, some guards won't let us up until we call someone inside to come escort us and sign for us like a delivered package; we may do this for others one day. Once past security, we might need the badge to enter our workspace, and it may not get us into others that we expect. This is true at client sites more than our at a place of permanent employment.

It is inevitable that we will go to work and forget our badge. Those who drive all the way to work can handle this by leaving it in the car, a much shorter retrace than all the way home. If we bring a bag, a purse, or lunch container nearly every day, this is another option. Find a solution before it happens. We can sometimes get a temporary badge issued for the day, but this can irritate some people, especially at client sites and worst of all at government ones.

The Water Cooler

Various sources of water exist at jobs: the water cooler, a fountain, refrigerator-supplied, and what we bring with us. The one that can cause trouble is the water cooler. These come in two varieties: those provided free, and those we must pay for the privilege of enjoying. We'll know if we must pay because a sign on or near it will tell us, and who to see about paying to join the water club. At a government agency, this person is almost always a government staff member due to being long term; turnover in this role isn't desired.

The liaison has a list of people in the club and whether they're up to date on dues. Joining is not a problem. Rather, not joining and using the water cooler anyway is what's frowned upon. We're stealing from everyone who is paying. Some do this because they are cheap, while others are bothered that they have to pay for water, given that we die without it. Some think an employer or client should supply it, and they aren't wrong. But what they are forgetting is that there's typically a working water fountain nearby, one that can fill a reusable container. They just don't want to use it for taste or hygiene reasons.

We should always pay to use the water cooler if it is required. The person organizing it is footing the bill for the whole thing unless people sign up for the club. The situation is not their fault. On the contrary, they have arranged this for people just like us and we should thank them *and* pay our dues.

Kitchens

Not all buildings have a kitchen available. Some don't even have a sink, and the "kitchen" is a table where someone has placed a microwave and a refrigerator beside it. Other buildings have a dedicated area or room with these and at least a sink, maybe one with a garbage disposal. At government buildings, we can seldom expect more than this. At private companies, there may be a nearly full kitchen, with a dishwasher, toaster, coffee machine, and large pantries for storage. Just don't expect a stovetop or wall oven. Only these fuller kitchens have seating, typically limited. This is a major reason we'll be eating at our desk.

Restaurants

Some buildings have a restaurant inside them. If not, there may be one within walking distance where it is still considered part of the building complex to which staff in our building have access. Some are open to the public like any eatery, but many are not, especially inside federally owned land with guards. What they all have in common is being like any restaurant: food is prepared there, we purchase it, and we can sit to eat, sometimes outside. Some such places do not allow outside food, but many do because they know most clientele are not the public, but the staff for whom the restaurant exists. Sometimes it is a working lunch, and while some are buying, others aren't. Many of them are a food court, which contributes to this.

Sometimes a chain like McDonald's exists, which was the case when I worked at NASA, the State Department, and the Pentagon. But a single business, or several, often runs each of the eateries just like we would see at a food court. Prices are comparable because they know we have other options.

Parking

For drivers, we should learn about our parking options during the hiring phase. This includes the availability of any parking and whether it's a garage, the street, and assigned (or forbidden/reserved) spaces. We may have to pay for it, fully or in part. If we are destined for client sites that change, there may be an allowance for parking; this is often not the full amount. There are sometimes exceptions that we may only learn about through coworkers. For example, at the State Department, even contractor motorcyclists could park under the building with a free permit, but otherwise only government people could.

We may notice coworker vehicles and their parking skills (or lack thereof) and car cleanliness. They may notice ours. We often have to provide our vehicle make, model, and license number to HR and this means that parking violations come to their attention. Clearly, we should avoid this. It is also wise to never leave the building without car keys (and the rest, like our house key), even for a fire alarm, because we may not get back in.

Since others can recognize our vehicle, and people are creatures of habit who often park in the same area, our absence from the office can lead to a glance out the window to see if we are there. This is yet another reason to ask our manager's permission to leave. A missing car also makes it easier to tell if other absent staff are just out of sight at the moment or left the building and drove away. What we can notice about others, they can notice about us. Don't let the absence come to manager attention and be a surprise to them.

Anecdote Time

Having lived near Washington D.C. most of my life, I knew parking garages were on nearly every street corner, but when I had an interview at the State Department's main D.C. building, I easily found nearby street parking instead. It came as no surprise when no street parking was available on my first day, but the total lack of parking garages across a wide swath of the area came as an unwelcome shock. From the Kennedy Center to the White House, and from the mall to a street farther north, there is nothing. Not one. I missed my first day because of it. Before I could start, I had to do a security briefing that I missed during my widening and fruitless search for somewhere to park. My client was understanding and amused; I was neither.

One employer couldn't interview me at their client's location because of security, so we did it at a nearby hotel. They said I could park there once hired and the company would cover the cost, as they did for the interview. They were wrong on both counts. After hiring, I worked at HQ instead of that site while awaiting my client badge, and I learned I had to park 15 minutes farther away for a shuttle that came every 15 minutes (I might just miss it), and ride it 15 minutes back. This was an additional 45 minutes, doubling my commute to 90 minutes, twice my acceptable limit. I resigned, and during the meeting where I told my understanding manager, I received the email telling me my badge had been approved and I could start at the client. I had dodged a bullet.

Office Relocations

Sometimes the company we're working for intends to switch buildings, floors, or areas, and that means everyone is losing their seat for another, which might be better or worse (everyone's fear). Management is typically aware that many become apprehensive about this for several reasons, including a dislike of change and the fear that we'll end up somewhere awful. Everyone is desperate to see the seating chart that is usually held under armed guard (kidding).

If we need a reason to be on good terms with management (our direct manager and everyone above them), this is at the top of the list. No one admits it, but people play favorites with seating assignments. Seniority often counts first on this, as does superior experience, but schmoozing skills are also a desirable commodity. Regardless of our eventual destination, try to handle it with good humor because the opposite—attitude—is a professional mistake.

CHAPTER FOUR

Social Events

Handling social gatherings at work is important to our survival. Not only do they provide an opportunity to improve our job situation, but a chance to worsen it. Most of us will navigate them fine without following specific advice, but being prepared and knowing what to expect never hurts, especially for those of us who are socially challenged.

There are three kinds of social events at work: the informal gatherings, the corporate sponsored ones, and those that lie somewhere in between. Every job will be different. It's best not to go in with any set expectations. Some coworkers are, too. Others might have a clique and we're not invited. We might be the only contractor (or one of a few) when everyone else is an employee and therefore we're a second-class citizen who isn't allowed to attend something.

Examples include:

- Corporate
    - Holiday parties (and cookouts/picnics)
    - Pizza/Bagel day
    - The softball team

- Informal
  - Getting coffee
  - Going to lunch
- The gray area
  - Welcome and farewell lunches
  - Birthday lunches
  - Baby showers

The informal events are ones where coworkers decide to do something together with no management involvement, approval, or funds spent. No permission is needed. This includes going to get coffee (regardless of what time of day) or lunch during work hours, whether or not that's on the clock. The corporate events are sanctioned by the CEO and involve corporate funds and official policies about attendance, guests, location, and whether time spent must be compensated for on our timesheet. Then there's the stuff that's in between, a gray area where corporate money may be spent but they're minimal, such as a birthday card or a welcome lunch, and management is involved in communication about it, but these are often optional and not a big deal.

Avoidance

The easiest solution to all of them is to avoid them, but this has one major drawback—it may seem that we don't like our coworkers or are not invested in our job. We can quickly gain a reputation for never showing up, with people joking about us, but as long as we're reasonably well liked, we can get a free pass. But if we're doing poorly at work or have an attitude, avoiding all social outings will have no one surprised when we quit—or are fired. It is arguably better to at least put in an appearance, usually at the start, and then leave early. This means we are accepting the hospitality, however briefly, instead of rejecting it.

Official Events

Some companies arrange for staff to get together over food and drink. These official events most often take place in the office during work hours (or right after) but can be offsite or on the weekend, when catering and a reserved place make them more important. The events that occur during work hours and at the office are hard to avoid without being obvious. The ones after work give us an excuse to leave, especially if commuting later will become a problem or we have children to pick up. The offsite events that are on the weekend come with built-in lack of attendance expectations, where no real excuse is needed. Regardless of time and location, these are always optional unless our manager explicitly commands us to attend, barring a good excuse.

They sometimes serve alcohol, often at no cost to us. There may be a two-drink limit, with two coupons given to us for this. Since this is a liability, it is more common at offsite events, like a holiday party. Even without a limit, we should not overindulge because of a host of mistakes that lie this way, from saying inappropriate remarks to flirting and worse. Holiday parties at a hotel have produced hookups and the occasional baby.

Try not to overeat, too. We can look like a pig or someone overly invested in consuming corporate benefits. If in a buffet line, try not to fill the plate to the brim. Along with others, we may end up shortchanging those at the back of the line. Be reasonable and circle back for seconds later instead. But if people arrive late and find all the food is gone, that is not on us.

For the events during work hours, companies will tell us if we need to make up the time or not. Sometimes the official policy is that we do, but no one does and our manager or peers may fill us in on that.

Some events involve sports: skiing, basketball, football, softball, volleyball, bowling, mini-golf (or the real deal), and lawn games like frisbee. If we are very competitive, we should dial that down because this is supposed to be friendly, not cutthroat, and that style may not go over well with office mates who are playing for fun and sometimes not in the best shape. Going all out can also cause injuries that may prevent future similar events, and we may be the person who ruined it for everyone else. Such activities can mean a change of clothes, with the planner remarking that this is okay. Just remember not to wear inappropriate sporting gear, like offensive slogans. We should avoid showing too much cleavage, gym shorts that cause a camel toe, or a tank top; no one wants to see our underarm hair.

In the Office

Due to how easy it is to attend onsite events, attending is wiser than skipping. We can schmooze and learn much about either coworkers or business developments that might affect us. At the least, we should "put in an appearance," coming for about ten minutes, snacking on something, and then discreetly leaving. Doing this at the start is better because of the mingling that often happens before the food line moves. It also creates the impression of being inclusive. If we wait until later, we often cannot undo the impression that we never showed up at all.

We can score points with the organizers by helping set up or clean up, but this isn't expected and the appreciation it creates doesn't last beyond a few days. They can also rebuff our offer to help set up because of the plans organizers have made; we just become a potential source of interference and another person they have to direct or overrule. But the cleanup offer almost never is. We can also just do it. This is a good last impression.

Offsite Corporate Parties

The economy can affect whether a company hosts an offsite party, but if one happens, there are additional considerations. The most frequent event is the holiday party near year's end; this can happen anytime between Thanksgiving into January, but they are seldom if ever on Christmas or New Year's Eve. They're also almost always on Friday or Saturday night. Other U.S. events include a July 4th or Labor Day picnic. Others might do something around Halloween or Thanksgiving.

Some companies restrict the event to staff, but we're often allowed to bring a date (or our children). The caution about getting inebriated applies to our guests. Make sure they understand this. We don't want to be embarrassed by their conduct. Be sure to include them in conversations or the occasion can be quite boring for them. Some workplaces are more like a clique than others. Keep in mind how shy your +1 is and help them as needed. And if there is tension between you, avoid showing it.

Informal Events

The Welcome Lunch

The first outing that we are likely to do may be within days. Coworkers may take us to lunch, with our manager possibly buying on the company dime; sometimes a person from HR will attend and take care of it. We should always assume we are paying for ourselves until told otherwise. This can be unclear. A phrase like "we are taking you to lunch," suggests they're buying, but if they say, "let's go to lunch," that does not. If there are no managers or HR reps, we are almost certainly paying. Try to read the situation, and if still in doubt when the check comes, pull out the wallet. If someone stops us, we say our thanks.

Sometimes another new staff member is being taken to lunch, and management asks us to join when we've been there a while; this is to make it more social. This usually means everyone is paying for themselves, except for the new person, but not always. Handle it the same. It's recommended to accept this offer to welcome that person this way because it creates a good impression. Sometimes several new people are taken to lunch at once and it is more likely that the company is buying for everyone.

Don't expect a welcome lunch outing. They rarely happen, officially or otherwise. For the first days, we may forgo bringing food just in case, then buying something nearby if it doesn't happen. We may choose not to eat early for a similar reason of having just eaten, only to be invited to lunch an hour later. If by the third day, it hasn't happened, it won't. The farewell lunch is even rarer and arguably reserved for truly beloved staff members, ones who've been around for years and are deeply connected, or those retiring.

Other Lunches

Coworkers sometimes decide to get lunch together. There isn't much to this, but we can be routinely left out without knowing why. A clique is one reason. Not clicking with the team is another. If we're the only one with our job function, or we are a consultant, they may never invite us. The latter implies we are not one of them and are only temporary anyway, so why include us? We may be invited and have no one talk to us the entire time. It can even be our welcome lunch, and yet we can be treated as if we are not present, there being no attention on us or questions about our background. The more tightknit the group we are with is, the more likely we are just an outsider. It is also possible to "perform" poorly at the first of these and not get a second chance. It is best not to take this personally, even if it is personal, but it will usually have more to do with our new peers and their social skills and inclusiveness than ours.

The Potluck

The potluck luncheon happens at many offices and is a scenario to navigate. The first concern is contributions. If we are attending, we should contribute. It's that simple. If we can't or don't want to cook, we can buy pre-made items like desserts, buns, chips, drinks and plastic cutlery. Some-one will have a list of what is already being brought and what may still be needed. We might bring in serving dishes or utensils, but these can sometimes go missing by accident. And if we still don't want to do even that, ask if a cash donation is accepted. We can also volunteer to help set up or breakdown.

For those who intend to cook, the food list can give us ideas on the sort of fare expected, but we can always ask. Potlucks are usually standard, with no strange foods. For example, a non-comprehensive list might include hot dogs, burgers (sometimes veggie or pork), chicken, wings, sweet meatballs, ham, turkey, chili, salad, mashed potato, potato salad, noodle salad, rolls, veggie tray, cooked vegetables, coleslaw, bottled water, sodas, chips/pretzels/dips, and various pies, cakes, cookies, and pastries.

Grilling at NASA

Some of these are BBQ items as there may be a grill, meaning we cook. As my contribution, I once grilled most of the burgers, hot dogs, and sausages for a 50-person pot-luck at NASA. This is something to do only if we are a seasoned griller, especially one who has already cooked for many people. One advantage to this role is that we will most likely be seen doing it, and it builds goodwill.

Unfamiliar foods don't do as well, so we should avoid bringing them. It is disheartening to see our dish still full because no one wants to eat it. Some people already feel that a potluck is risky because so many people are preparing food and we question how fastidious our cooking coworkers are; this is one reason some people don't take part at all. Bringing food that looks weird or unusual is a poorer choice.

Some items are much easier to bring than others. At one extreme is prepackaged food tossed into a bag. At the other is a crockpot with contents that should be made the day before and must be reheated after carefully transporting them in our car so that it doesn't spill. Choose wisely and don't make this harder than it needs to be unless truly motivated. Those new to corporate life may be wise to avoid cooking.

Getting Coffee

While some bring coffee or similar drinks to work, others get them after arriving or several times a day. They may invite us to come and we should at least sometimes go to be social. We don't need to buy a coffee if we don't drink it. Tea or pastries may be available, too. The coffee run could be within the office or a walk or drive to a nearby place. If we leave the office, this is not work time, but we often get away with it provided we don't go overboard. Besides, we can talk about work, treating it like an impromptu walking meeting, even though no one discusses the job. Our manager may do it, too, and they usually wave this off as social bonding without ever saying so.

Happy Hours

As expected, happy hour is always after work and is not a job function. What can surprise us is that we may have no idea people are doing this. This comes up if we have an early work schedule, leaving by 3-4 PM, with happy hour typically starting at 5-6 PM. If we want to be included, we may need to adjust our schedule, but we first need to find out if it is even happening. This can be tough if it's a clique and we aren't in it, because they may not want to tell us. We should also be the sort who is good in bars. If we're a quiet talker, it may not be the best venue for us. We also need to watch our alcohol intake.

Talking Points

There are subjects we should avoid at work because they are too emotionally charged or too personal. Politics and religion are two. So are intolerant views on sexuality, gender, and minorities. Even if we are tolerant, we should avoid these topics because someone around us might be intolerant and it can lead to uncomfortable feelings or conversations. HR sometimes has policies forbidding certain subjects.

Some will say this infringes on freedom of speech, but that right in the United States is about the government restricting that freedom. We most likely work for a public or private company, where this freedom doesn't exist. Besides, voluntarily deciding not to discuss certain things is not about freedom—it's about professional courtesy, not airing an attitude, and not triggering one in someone else. People lose jobs for those.

We should also not discuss our personal life overly much or at all, depending on the subject. Where we went for vacation is fine, but our divorce details or family problems are not. Nor are past or current professional problems if they give a negative impression of us. So are any abusive or legal situations we have been in, or ones involving illegal substances, or even legal ones when we overindulged. We must also not comment on the appearance of coworkers (or anyone else). If we wouldn't say it during an interview, on the job is no better.

There are many such unwelcome topics that fall under "common sense," but people run afoul of this anyway. Be smart and take a cue from those around you, unless they veer into these subjects. It is okay to excuse yourself from the conversation.

On the other end are positive events like our impending wedding or childbirth, both of which we can (and likely should) admit without reservation; not admitting to them would be odd, even off-putting. Any achievement is a suitable subject, provided we aren't bragging. We want to share just enough of who we are and our lives that people feel some connection to us and that we aren't an empty shell they know nothing about. If we hit it off with someone, then we go deeper.

Getting to know people at work can benefit our job satisfaction, even for the most anti-social among us. This includes letting peers get to know us at least a little. Sports teams, TV shows, films, and similar light fare are good for showing some personality while keeping a cool distance, if we are not comfortable sharing more. We don't have to be tightlipped. A little bit of sharing goes a long way to being included and seeming inclusive ourselves, and it makes office life smoother.

At some jobs, people make no attempt at including us in their conversations despite inviting us to come along for something like coffee. They may discuss ongoing subjects or ones that we may not know much about. We can feel that while our presence was requested, our input was not. This is not to say anyone is doing this on purpose so much as like being a "third wheel." It is awkward and the only thing we can really do is try to find opportunities to chime in. This can be especially difficult if we know little about the subject, but that gives us a chance to ask. Some persistence is key. Join in, or this invitation might be the last.

Anecdote Time

One of my employer's clients created the most awkward working experience of my career. They pretended I didn't exist the entire 40-hour work week, for the six months that I was there. Even the receptionist wouldn't say hello or make eye contact. The staff did their Thanksgiving lunch in the office and were so close to my cube while dining that I could not get out of it. Someone's chair blocked me in. They did not invite me. When presented with an opportunity to work from home once a week, I took it. Then I had the chance to work back at my employer's office for another two days a week. Same. When finding ourselves in such a situation, we can try to befriend people only to learn we cannot enter the clique, so it is best to bear this with good grace.

Birthday Celebrations

Some would say that celebrating or acknowledging birthdays is best left out of the corporate world. We're not children anymore. And no one cares. Some are trying to forget they're another year older. But many companies, or groups within them, think otherwise, and they may pull us into this. HR already knows our birthday and may be responsible for recognitions, but others sometimes champion this. There are several options for these birthday recognitions, whether ours or someone else's.

The Card

The simplest is the birthday card that someone buys with company funds. They will place this in a non-descript folder that makes the rounds at work. Sometimes there is a sheet inside with everyone's name on it. They expect us to check off our name that we signed the card so that the folder doesn't return to us, then sign the card. Definitely do the former. The latter is not truly necessary if we don't want to, but a signature is all that is required (no cute message, which everyone who hasn't seen the card yet will see). When we are done, it is now our job to take the folder to someone who has not checked off their name, or return to the person in charge of this. All the while, we are supposed to prevent the ultimate recipient from seeing this folder so it can be a surprise.

The Lunch

Some managers will take the birthday boy or girl out for lunch. They will use the corporate credit card. They may invite others to attend at their own expense, and it's usually everyone in a definable group so that they leave no one out. They might ask us to pick the restaurant if we're the guest of honor. People can come to expect this on seeing it happen for others, but this can be a problem if they bypass us, whether on purpose or not. This is one reason the practice isn't wise.

If we are not the guest of honor, we don't have to attend, but not doing so can look personal. Instead of openly declining, it can be prudent to make ourselves scarce at the time that people are gathering to leave, as they will carpool, and if we are a no-show, they only wait so long. Avoidance is a skill of survival.

The Cake

If there's a gathering aside from lunch, it is typically so the card can be given to the person and for a cake and light refreshments. This is rare and usually for important managers, VPs, and above. Feel free to skip this, but given the rank of those for whom it occurs, putting in an appearance may be wise. We shouldn't be surprised if someone comes by our desk and asks if we want some cake. This is partly to include us, so be gracious about declining. There is also an assumption that everyone loves and wants cake, so if we don't have any, maybe we didn't realize it was happening. They are being thoughtful. Savor it. Thoughtfulness at work can be rare.

Baby Showers

When someone is expecting a baby, sometimes people at work arrange a baby shower. This is true for both men and women, though women arguably get this more because of the physical signs of pregnancy. The same person responsible for birthdays will probably come around with a card (like birthdays; see that section for details). They may ask for baby gift donations via cash. We should contribute; if we can't give a new life something positive to get going, when can we give? I could make the case that we're also buying a positive attitude toward ourselves.

During the baby shower, the gifts are given and there is usually at least a cake if not some other minor food. These events last 30-60 minutes during work time. We don't have to show up, but doing so shows good will. We likely signed the card and this can be a "get out of baby shower free" card. We have options. Choose one that shows some support even if you couldn't care less. One day you might be an expecting parent and appreciate the gesture.

Who is Driving?

If we are headed to lunch, coffee, or another social outing, and the destination isn't within walking distance, this usually means we'll be piling into someone's car. This is a personal item and we therefore should make a positive comment or say nothing; never criticize unless you know them well. If the owner jokes or apologizes about a mess, the "no worries" type of response is expected. If someone is tall, let them have the front passenger seat, but if we're the tall one, we can politely request it, such as by asking, "Anyone mind if I take the front because of my height?"

They will not expect us to drive on the first of these trips because we may not know where we are going. We should pay attention so that we know how to get there next time, then offer to drive at another invitation. Be prepared with a car that is at least a little cleaned up. When the trip is over, "Thanks for driving" is wise.

Bring Your Kid to Work Day

Many countries take part in "Bring Your Kid to Work Day." Our workplace may not, but if it does, we should find out when this is to be prepared. It's not that we must really do anything other than expect some distraction, but this is usually minor. Parents have admonished their children to behave well and keep quiet, like it's a library. We sometimes forget that the kids are around, they can be so well behaved.

If we want to avoid them and have the option to work from home, we might request it for that day. When parents bring their children in, it is often for only a few hours, as the kids won't survive the entire day any more than some adults would. They get bored, even with electronic devices to amuse them. Parents who want to do this have likely seen this before and already know what to expect by the time it's our turn to bring a child in. The day becomes a half-day for the parents, or they work from home for the rest of it, so those who are dreading this experience may worry unnecessarily.

CHAPTER FIVE

Personal Time

We may be at work, but they do not expect us to work every second. Chatting with coworkers is one example of a time that is technically unproductive, but which is normal. There is also an assumption that this came up while we were talking to them about actual business and is not the primary reason we're talking. This is something to keep in mind. Sneak in the chit chat; don't frequently make it the whole point of a conversation. None of this is really personal time, however. We'll look at several items that are.

Being Monitored

First, a word about being watched.

Our employer can observe computer use in at least two ways: someone sees our screen, or the network engineering team responsible for setting up and maintaining our work computer monitors it. Both happen and they may state the latter in an employee handbook. Whether anyone has the time to monitor us is one thing, but website traffic logs can be stored for later perusal if someone gets the impression we are slacking and maybe frivolous internet use is the reason, so they investigate our computer history. It is best to assume someone is watching not for paranoia, but self-preservation. The phrase "everything in moderation" applies here. If we don't go overboard, we are usually fine. This comes with the caveat to not view porn, gamble, or conduct a business, as three examples of inappropriate computer work; more will be spelled out in the handbook.

It also bears mentioning that the invention of the smartphone has made using our work computer for anything internet-related unnecessary. Sure it's got a smaller screen, but there is seldom a reason to check email or much of anything else via the company computer. "Avoidance is a skill of survival," and in this case, that means don't take unnecessary risks. If we connect our smartphone to the company network, we can be monitored.

There are keystroke monitoring apps that can run on our computer with or without our awareness. Most companies don't do this, but federal government agencies are more likely to, especially in the defense industry (army, navy, etc.). There is once again the question of whether anyone has time to be checking. This is a reason to never log in to personal email such as Gmail from work computers; they can see our password.

They can also monitor our physical presence, though this is typically via observation, not surveillance. Access cards will record when we enter, but only if we swipe them, so consistent tardiness can be noticed and verified this way. Not swiping happens when we piggyback on someone else having swiped, or an exiting person holding the door for us. Some companies insist this not happen, and yet people do it anyway out of politeness and indifference to the policy.

We want to avoid the appearance of long absences from the building or our desk. Tell someone when off at a meeting. Appearances matter and someone getting suspicious only to learn we had a valid excuse doesn't help us as much as we might think. They still suspected us of not working and that only goes away so much once exonerated. Avoid it ahead of time. The same is true of offsite meetings, or a doctor's appointment that requires us to make it up. Being upfront about it is golden.

Wasting Time

Wasting time at work is a fact of life, including in the corporate world, though many companies won't admit that staff do it. The real problem for us is ensuring our employer doesn't think we're doing it. "Perception is reality" means that if people think we are not working, we're not. Never mind that we are. We can lose our job over this and other interpretations that are wrong; by the time we know this, it is too late.

We must always get our work done by a deadline or keep our manager aware of slippage as soon as we are certain it will happen; and we will want to clearly explain why it's happening. They don't like being surprised when the deadline is missed any more than we like them assuming we were goofing around instead of working.

Be aware that if we routinely turn in work before it is due, this can give the impression that we aren't being given enough work and more will come our way, possibly overloading us. We might think they'll decide we're a hard worker, but we cannot control their interpretation and consistently being done early can backfire. It is at these moments that we might be tempted to briefly socialize with coworkers, which can improve both our morale and theirs, but be mindful that their work may not be done yet and when they explain to their manager the reason for missing their deadline, that the reason shouldn't be that we were hanging out with them all the time.

Our manager may ask us to estimate how long something will take us to complete. Providing accurate estimates is easier with more work experience and we should strive for it. When giving such an estimate, ask for feedback or at least gauge the reaction ours estimate receives. Sometimes a manager makes an estimate for us. If they suggest a significantly shorter amount of time, we will need to explain why we think more hours are needed.

More seasoned workers may find another opportunity to make work less stressful by padding the estimate, within reason. If we think it will take two days, we can say two-and-a-half, but saying it will take five is a mistake, especially if our manager used to do what we do or otherwise knows better. Some professions require more leeway, such as software development, where bugs and other unforeseen issues arise. This can make padding especially wise so that we aren't behind all the time.

The Holy Trinity of Goofing Off is working alone, having no required status reports, and our manager not paying attention even when we try to tell them the latest updates to our work. The implication is that this is great, but losing this job altogether is more likely than others because management may assume we aren't doing anything. It is especially important to proactively make it clear that we are making progress. Even simple management unawareness of activities suggests there *aren't* any activities.

Computer Work

Virtually all corporate jobs involve significant computer use. We are supposed to only use this for our job, of course, but people do various unrelated activities on the company's computers. It is wise to remember that anything we create there technically belongs to owner of the machine, or even to the client if we are billing our time to one. This means that if we write a novel while at work, we don't own it, and if our activity is discovered and the company takes us to court over the copyright, they would win. Few of us are novelists, but there are other personal activities that fall into the same category. Forbidden activities can cause immediate termination and possible legal action; these behaviors could result in money being made, which means we are doing business for ourselves on company time, an act explicitly forbidden in employment contracts.

One way we can be caught doing such things is that we will have to transfer the file off that work computer eventually. Uploading it via Google drive, for example, or even to a personal email account, means it goes across the company network, possibly being stored indefinitely along the way. Even if we create such a document in cloud storage so that it was always there and never on the company network, keystroke capture or screen capture software can reveal our activity. As with many things, moderation is key; typing a few notes to ourselves is usually fine, but the next chapter of our novel is not.

For those moments of jotting down notes to ourselves, our personal smartphone is the best choice for privacy. Since no one would write a novel on one, we also get the benefit of the doubt that whatever we're doing is just a minute or two, not the full day that our example novel chapter would take. As a personal device, it lies beyond corporate inspection, though some companies will state otherwise. That may not hold up in court, but we don't want to put ourselves anywhere near a position to find out by not getting our work done and arousing suspicion.

We may feel justified in doing some personal work if we have purposely worked hard and fast to get our company work done ahead of schedule, precisely so that we can spend a few minutes on a personal item. Be aware that such an excuse will not be viewed favorably. It still behooves us to not be open about it. The funny thing is that we could spend many minutes chatting about non-work items with a coworker and get a free pass, but doing personal work on the computer can cause termination. What they have in common is not performing work for our job, but they are viewed quite differently, and we must be aware of the risks we take.

Regardless of your choice, always get work done first. And remember that just because no one has said anything to us about it doesn't mean they didn't notice.

Always lock the computer when stepping away. This prevents intrusion into our work. In some companies, and especially government agencies, failing to do this is a security violation and we can get in trouble. If we have non-work related things on screen like Amazon.com on Prime Day, it is easier for someone to check this out when we're gone. Even when doing our work, we don't want others commenting unnecessarily on how we perform our duties with our screen arrangement or anything else. Some pranksters also like to alter things for us, and someone more nefarious could send an email from our computer in our absence, with us punished. Lock the computer.

Watching Videos

Since it is possible to watch movies and TV shows online, it can be tempting to do this at work. Some of us can work better this way if we are doing boring and repetitive computer work, so it being a distraction that slows us down is not necessarily true. And it may be no more distracting than our surroundings; it can even stop those distractions. But as is often true in life, perception is more important than reality, so if we are seen watching something, this will be frowned upon.

If we choose to do it, we don't want the bandwidth noticed by our employer, so do not use the company network for it. This means not watching video on the work computer. Some services have an app where we can download items to our phones while at home using our Wi-Fi and then watch it later. As usual, it is imperative that we get our work done on schedule. Do not use video unless it actually promotes higher quality and speed. We must know ourselves and be honest to gauge this. Even then, do not be seen doing it.

Errands

Running errands while we're supposed to be working is best done quickly, meaning a detour of under ten minutes if we are already outside the building for something like an offsite meeting or lunch. We once again do not want to lie about this. For example, we could try to cite traffic to explain a delay in returning, but what if someone from work is doing a similar errand in the same place and sees us? This is one reason to do it during lunch, where we are just doing the pit-stop because we were nearby anyway. Just spend the extra minutes at work that afternoon to make up the time. And be very visual about doing so. It's advisable to just admit to the desire to do it and ask permission, offering to make up time, than to try being sneaky about it.

Phone Calls

Personal phone calls at work are part of life and most managers understand this. We can do it if we don't go overboard in frequency or duration. Or discuss items too sensitive for work; people are going to overhear our half of the conversation. Regardless of content or length, it's often best to walk away from our desk on our mobile phone. There is little reason to use the work phone. A hallway is good for a quick, undramatic call. Anything else is better farther away.

This includes outside or in an unused area of work, should one exist; some buildings have deserted areas where no one sits. Being seen in such places has one side effect: it is clear we are there on purpose, planned it, and may sometimes be there instead of at our desk. All of this can raise suspicion to mitigate with brevity or letting our manager know we need to make a quick call. We can also arouse suspicion if going to a floor of the building where no one expects us to be, but can discover us without warning. By contrast, stepping outside can be done for multiple reasons and is therefore more innocent in appearance, such as someone calling us when we were already there.

Another activity is the walk. Even before FitBit and similar devices, every job had the walkers—people who do laps for exercise or just to not sit all day. No one begrudges this activity, though it is implied that we will make up that time at our desk. Some people do this inside depending on the building layout, making laps in the hallways. But doing it outside with earbuds in and the phone in our pocket means that a casual look at us suggests we are just walking a bit. This is one way to disguise we are taking a longer personal call, should we desire to, but it doesn't really matter because in either case, we must make up the time; and it always pays to be upfront about our activity.

Email

With the invention of smartphones, there is seldom if ever a reason to log in to personal email on a work device. Traffic sent across the network can be intercepted and read. Reading or sending personal emails this way is easy to avoid. Equally important is not to use the company's email client, such as Microsoft Outlook, for personal email. It is automatically their business to read. It may be fine to email ourselves a file or notes, for example, but assume someone is reading this and don't do it if concerned about that. Sending ourselves work files could technically be frowned upon, even to work on them at home via a personal computer as work time, so be careful with that as well.

Anecdote Time

A Vice President once emailed me to come to her office, and when I arrived, she was in a heated argument with a coworker of mine. Using his work computer and personal Gmail account, he had emailed someone about the work he was doing. This had allowed the employer to snoop, and they were not happy with whatever he had written. But the argument was solely about their right to do this. Incensed, he said they had violated his privacy. She disagreed (and she was right). I swore I would never use a personal email account from work again and have not.

Part Two

It Ends

CHAPTER SIX

Threats to Our Job

There are many reasons our job can end, from quitting on good terms to being fired and everything in between. We'll look at a few scenarios.

Our Manager's Opinion

It will come as no surprise that our manager's opinion of us can cost us our job. Societies promote the idea that doing excellent work leads to advancement, because without it, we have far less motivation to do well. And yet, sometimes this isn't true for several reasons. One of those is that our personal traits might conflict with those of our manager. Assessing our manager's personality is therefore one of our most important survival skills. There is no special secret to this. We mostly need to watch how they handle situations.

For example, if we make a suggestion for improvement, is it implemented? Do we receive a genuine "That's a good idea" or do they frown or make a disapproving remark? This can tell us whether showing initiative is appreciated or can get us into trouble. Either way, we should make suggestions because we're trying to improve things for the company, and not give the impression we're suggesting it because we want to be rewarded for it.

Another big reveal is when we bring a problem to their attention. Do they tell us to grow up, to just deal with it, to solve it ourselves? Maybe they sound like they really don't want to hear about it. This could be innocent in that they have too many other issues to deal with, but even in that scenario, they should be professional about it. Otherwise, it can suggest they don't care about the impact of blowing us off—we might not bring items to their attention.

With problems we bring them, it is wise to suggest a solution so that we are proactive and positive; raising an issue is inherently negative. But as we already discussed, showing initiative can be frowned upon. Ultimately, what we're looking for is their attitude when interacting with us. A negative attitude is something that we, and they, should never show. This is precisely why it is revealing of our standing with our manager if he or she shows an attitude to us or another subordinate. This might not be someone who values or respects their staff, and this can lead to many issues that threaten our job.

When we do well, a manager who gives even small kudos is better than many alternatives. Sometimes our achievement is disregarded as nothing more than doing our job, even if we did extra effort. Being taken for granted is a red flag suggesting this manager won't appreciate us. Worse is when they resent an outstanding job performance. This is often a sign of an insecure boss, which is one of the more perilous traits in the workplace; it reverses perceptions, such as excelling suggesting to them that we're ambitious and want our supervisor's job, so they feel threatened.

There are far too many scenarios to cover, but there are several ways to learn our manager's opinion of us: they tell us, someone else does, or we guess using clues. Let's examine each.

They Tell Us

Our manager telling us their assessment typically occurs during a performance review, if we ask, or if we have made a big enough mistake/achievement that they brought us into a meeting.

At a Performance Review

The performance review is a challenging aspect of employment; consultants and contractors are spared these. Early in our careers, we assume that doing well results in a positive review and vice versa, but this isn't always true. We can mitigate issues here with some awareness and proactivity, though no advice is foolproof.

A surprisingly positive assessment is a rarity. We usually know these are coming, but we may expect one and find ourselves disappointed. Even when we've done well, they can bring issues to our attention, some more warranted than others. If we see that they have a point, it is wise to admit it, thank them for pointing it out, and try to take the high road while assuring them we'll work on it. Responding this way can also work if we disagree, but this is hard.

There are multiple reasons managers may give us a performance review that underwhelms us. The most innocent is that they literally forgot the quality or quantity of our work during the past year; reviews are typically annual. Supervisors manage multiple people, and the larger their team, the more likely they are to forget regarding each individual's performance. Keep a list of your achievements as they accumulate. Learn when managers are expected to deliver performance reviews and assume they work on them up to a month prior. We want to remind them of our accomplishments before they write our review (when it is too late).

The meeting where we receive the review is not a discussion about what they're intending to write. It is a verdict, one that they may have shown their supervisor and HR. That can cause it to be "officially" signed off on, especially if a bonus or discipline is to occur; they often mention this. Waiting until the review takes place means our input is too late to affect the review, and this is crucial when the review is "wrong."

Before sending a list of accomplishments to our manager, we may want to casually mention that we want to. Don't make it seem like a big deal; they can interpret that as worry or thinking they're too stupid to remember, as two examples. Ask permission, such as, "Hey would it be okay for me to send you an updated list of the projects I've done over the last year? I know you get status reports, but a lot of it was a long time ago. Even I don't remember and will have to look through my notes when I'm on break." If this is handled well, they will appreciate it. Know your manager and adjust your tone accordingly.

Another reason for an underwhelming review is that managers may be directed to not dole out praise. Bonuses may be tied to them and the company may not want to grant them at this time. Some managers can believe that staff perform better to earn praise, which should therefore be withheld to keep us motivated; and yet they can fail to realize that not acknowledging staff who have already excelled causes resentment that makes them work less. This may not be our immediate manager's viewpoint, but someone above them or in HR providing direction.

They can also encourage managers to say something negative for similar rationalizations. One is giving us an area to improve on. This can cause them to exaggerate a non-issue into a supposed problem. This nitpicking can create an impression that they dislike us; not taking a review personally is an art form, and it pays to view it in context of the overall relationship.

One way to mitigate all of this is to purposely make a specific mistake, so that this is what our manager brings up. This can inhibit them looking for other, essentially made-up reasons to give us grief. We can almost do them a favor by making it easy for them to criticize something of our choosing. Be careful with this and choose something trivial, such as being one minute late to some meetings (not the ones where the CEO is coming). But even this can grow out of control if we have fallen out of favor.

Anecdote Time

At an early job, I seldom performed work for my immediate manager because I was a software developer who had only been assigned to him because I sat near him (yes, really). He knew nothing of software development and had no such projects. Every week, my status report to him listed the work I had done for other managers, departments, or projects; my timesheets, which he signed, also reflected the allocation of my hours to those items. Imagine my surprise when, at my performance review, he accused me of doing nothing.

I reminded him of one project after another, to which he sheepishly admitted, one by one, that he had forgotten about them. He chuckled. I relaxed. The disapproving attitude toward me, and the tension in the room, vanished. And then I asked how long it would take to rewrite my performance review. He looked startled, laughed, and said he couldn't do that because his manager had already signed off on it. The tension reappeared as he admitted he was sticking me with a bad review that he knew was wrong. The likely reason was that it would make him look bad to his manager, that he had forgotten all of my work, and he chose to make me look bad rather than taking any responsibility or blame for himself. I asked HR about this and was told I could write a response to it for my file, so I did. While this rebuttal can be good, it is uncommon and can be easily disregarded, so we must not place all faith in being able to do so. Ensure management knows your achievements.

At another employer, I was told that not bringing a notepad to meetings was a sign I didn't care about my job. He did not *ask* me why I didn't bring one, so I explained that the meetings were to give him status, and I did not need notes to remember what I had done that week, nor did he respond with anything I needed to write down. I nonetheless brought a notepad from then onward and wrote notes I didn't need.

Because We Asked

Asking our manager what he or she thinks of us is tricky because it can seem needy. Are we always going to be asking how we're doing? If we lack confidence, maybe they shouldn't give us great assignments or put us in positions of importance. Maybe they should let us go if downsizing is happening soon. We cannot control how others view our actions, so use this sparingly and with focus.

For example, rather than a general question, "How am I doing?", ask something specific. If we are giving them documentation we've written, we might ask when doing so, "Please let me know if there's anything else I should tweak about this." This makes the feedback about the work, not about us, and such feedback is expected and probably coming anyway. Commentary about how we're doing is not normal except at performance review time, and this is part of why we don't ask for it outside of that.

When we ask for feedback about us (not our work), we can make them find things to criticize. Some will want to avoid giving praise unnecessarily and therefore not give us the reassurance we might be seeking. Some may say everything is great when it's not because they dislike conflict. They may not want to say anything bad in a situation that is not under their control; a performance review is when they are calling the shots, not an impromptu question from us. At a review, their guard is up and they've had a chance to carefully frame their remarks. On the fly questions put them on the spot and may not be viewed favorably.

Ask for feedback on your work, not yourself.

When We Make a Big Mistake

We will quickly learn our manager's opinion of us when they discover a big mistake of ours. The judgement will not be about only our work, but us. Can they expect us to repeat such blunders again? If so, we might not be long for the job. This will not wait for our performance review. Instead, we will get a meeting request. If HR or anyone more important than our manager sends it, we may have reason to fear for our jobs. This may also be true if those people are present when we enter the room.

This is the most awful way to learn what management thinks. Even if they don't terminate us, they may negatively view much of what we do from now on so that we need to walk on eggshells. Assess how much peril the job is in— and how much extra scrutiny you will tolerate. This can last months or even years, and we will not know how long the black cloud will last. Relationships sour at work just as they do in any other place.

The only proper solution to this is avoiding mistakes and even excelling, but this may not be enough. How liked we are can affect this. They can negatively view a disliked employee who does skilled work while a liked but incompetent one sails past trouble. This is one reason sucking up to management is popular. Determine how well you fit in to get a sense of the potential duration of your black cloud.

Someone Else Tells Us

Someone other than our manager can tell us what our supervisor thinks. Praise may come this way, but usually praise comes directly from the manager; few other people feel comfortable giving it. By contrast, badmouthing others behind their back is more common for several reasons. People like to complain about something (or someone), doing it to our face is uncomfortable, and many like to gossip. If they sense others dislike us and will enjoy criticism of us, we may be inviting them to do it. Others will reward them. Never mind that witnesses will realize it can be done to them, too. Many don't seem to know or care about this.

Most people try to stay out of such things, so even a good work friend may not tell us negative comments our manager made about us. The supervisor might know better than to do it in front of them, too, knowing that we're friends. Learning our manager's opinion from someone else seldom happens. We gain far more by observation.

Assessing Our Manager

If we don't ask our manager's opinion and no one tells us, we must guess. This is the most common method of assessing it. We will interact many times in a week, maybe even each day, and each instance tells us something. This includes trivial things like how genuine their greeting or smile is, whether they laugh at a joke we make, or comments like "I trust you" or "thanks." These can be powerful indications of good or ill will. We first need to establish a baseline of how they usually interact so that we can assess changes to this. This is based on patterns of behavior lasting weeks. When things change, we also need new patterns, as a single instance of anything is seldom enough to know of a change in the winds. This is true in all aspects of relationships, not just at work.

If we can hang out with our manager in an informal setting, like lunch, we should. It is a chance to learn what else is going on in their lives and which may impact their mood. This can also lead us astray, however. Maybe they did indeed have a change of heart about us for the worse, but we learn they have a personal trouble and disregard the demeanor shift toward us. Nothing is foolproof and we must trust our instincts but not make too big a deal of them. If we are truly on shaky ground, we won't need to guess how we are viewed because one of the other methods will arise.

People have lives outside of ourselves. They can have a bad day for reasons that have nothing to do with us. We can have one before even seeing them. Sadly, many people forget this and often take things personally. It is one reason to never show frustration or other negative attitudes while at work. Many will just assume it is about them and can grow to dislike us or decide we have an attitude. Even when they know something terrible is going on in our personal lives, they may not cut us any slack.

Not all managers (or other staff) are reasonable. While former honor students end up in positions of authority in the corporate world, so do the below average people and everyone in between. Many are incompetent, lazy, insecure, overly sensitive, prideful, or have other faults that might become apparent while working for them. When realizing our manager has such traits, we must strive not to ignore them and, God forbid, we certainly cannot comment on them. But even a knowing, judging look can get us on their bad side. Pointing out a manager's mistake, even if we help them prevent others from seeing it, can be the fast track to problems. This is a reason even making suggestions can be viewed poorly—we are implying something isn't good enough, and for all we know, our manager is responsible for the item we are implicitly criticizing.

Sucking up to Management

All of this contributes to some people trying to curry favor with management. A truly egregious error spares no one, but milder issues may do less damage if we are well liked. Sucking up is best done carefully and naturally so that we do not appear to be doing it. Otherwise, it seems disingenuous and manipulative, and can backfire. Doing something like offering to help with something when you overhear them say that they are very busy is smooth and natural, as opposed to just doing it without circumstances prompting it.

Personal compliments are to be avoided, but making chit chat is typically beneficial in establishing and maintaining rapport. If they discuss their personal life, try to show interest but keep a neutral distance. It depends on the topic—their impending divorce is too personal, but if they're discussing helping their kid with a school project, this is safer. Their personal life is for them to raise, not us. What is easier is anything like a sporting event, TV show, or other conversation starter (but seldom politics). Clues may abound in their office paraphernalia and provide a chance to innocently raise the subject either at the start or end of a conversation. There are many ways to do this; just use your life skills for bonding with someone.

But it will all be for nothing if we aren't doing our job.

Looking for Another Job

Another threat to our job is our search for another one. It may seem odd that an employer might fire us because we are thinking of leaving, but it happens. Sometimes we are not actually looking, but they think we are, and so they fire us. This has happened to me twice (in a row). Why do companies do this? Several reasons.

One is an assumption that an unhappy employee is unproductive, so why should they pay us to do poor or even non-existent work? While there can be truth to this, it also assumes that we are unprofessional. Or does it assume we are human? Many people are eager to leave on good terms and work hard right until the end, but when our employer fires us this way, it does the opposite. Now we're leaving on awful terms, are unemployed, and we probably don't think highly of our now former employer. Would we ever go back? Probably not. They have shoved us out the door and burned the bridge while we were still standing on it.

Spite is another reason. Some people take an employee's departure personally, as if we are rejecting them. This can be true, but there is every likelihood that it is the job and not personal. If we have already determined that our supervisor is immature and thinks everything is about them, this could be a higher probability. If they don't like us or there's tension, this can make them cut us loose. And if they were already thinking of terminating us regardless of reason, it is virtually guaranteed.

If we have a major life change, such as moving across the country and teleworking isn't an option, or making a career switch, we may receive a better response if they learn we're going to leave. The only reason is that they don't take it personally. But don't count on this. We should always be prepared to be terminated without warning, even when we are not looking to go.

For these reasons (and likely more), we should be discreet when searching for new jobs. This includes taking phone calls and doing interviews, maybe even receiving text messages that appear on our phone while we have stepped away and someone can see it. Keep the phone with you to prevent the latter. Do not make or take calls from recruiters unless it is to schedule another time to talk. An exception is if we have stepped away from work, and the hallway does not count. A coworker can come by or overhear us, even around a corner. Leave the office space altogether.

Interviews can be tricky if done in person, as they are almost always during work hours for either us or the potential employer. We should only tell our manager we have an appointment and not specify why. But one potential issue is many appointments that might make them wonder and snoop, or jump to conclusions. Having kids can help us with this because they are a great excuse, but this seldom applies to the twenty-something staff. Either way, schedule conversations before work, after, or during lunch hours. If we normally work 7-3, getting this in after work is easier without ever letting our job know. But sometimes we have little choice. Virtual and phone interviews provide more flexibility, especially if we can work from home, in which case the commuting time saved allows us to schedule these before and after work.

Another issue with in-person interviews is the potential need to dress nicer than we do for work. This can be a reason to sometimes do this anyway. For example, dark slacks can go with a suit or without, but khakis do not. Therefore, don't always wear khakis. For men, we need the jacket, tie, and button-up shirt for the interview, so we can leave the first two in the car and just put them on when we reach our interview. On days when we don't have an interview, the dark pants and shirt are just one of our normal outfits and don't arouse suspicion. But don't hang the jacket in the car or park near known coworker vehicles; we don't want someone to see it. Women have greater flexibility to wear something nice without people thinking they are interviewing, but it again means occasionally dressing this way long before we have interviews.

On some job boards, we can have our resume "active" so that employers can find us more easily. The problem is that our current employer can see we have done this. On Monster.com, we once could block them, but this feature is gone as of this writing. We instead must list our resume as "anonymous," and this supposedly obscures the name of our current employer besides our personal details. This is not a great option because, in my experience, fewer contacts from recruiters result. This can be a good reason to keep a list of recruiters who have reached out to us in the past and follow up with them now, sending a current resume.

Anecdote Time

I once worked for Company XYZ, which had its own recruiters. But one owner had a second, smaller Company 123 that had none, so XYZ did recruiting for 123, too. On the job boards, I blocked XYZ from being able to see my resume, but the same people had an account on the boards via Company 123 and saw my resume was active. My manager fired me, told me that I was disloyal, and said he'd thrown me under the bus all the way up to the CEO and that protesting by going over his head would not get me anywhere. He then had the audacity to ask me if there was anything he could do for me while I was cleaning out my desk. Such a company probably isn't where we want to be working anyway. One plus here is that unemployment offices can side with us in a dispute because being fired for job searching is not misconduct; future employers are typically sympathetic as well.

Two-Week Notice

Quitting by giving our manager two-week's (i.e., ten full working days) notice is standard practice but not mandatory, even if our employer says it is in their employee handbook. Such a "requirement" is because they want us to depart in such a way that we don't cause any problems by not handing over our work, for example. Companies cannot enforce this, though it may depend on jurisdiction.

Even if we don't really need to do it, we should always try to. The adage about not burning bridges behind us applies. We may want to return or get a reference. We might even end up working with soon-to-be former coworkers at other companies one day. Some will say we can get a poor reputation by not giving adequate notice, and while it may be true, such advice has seldom stopped companies from firing someone immediately upon receiving two-week notice (giving themselves a bad reputation). This suggests there's a double standard where they can do the wrong thing and not be badmouthed for it, but we must do the "right" thing or face consequences. To each his own, but don't skimp on this unless truly necessary.

On giving notice, we should be prepared to be fired. But this is the best excuse for a firing. Neither an unemployment office nor potential employer will frown upon *us* if we say we gave two-week notice and they fired us immediately. Just as we discussed under a previous heading about "Looking for Another Job," spite and similar reasons can lead to this, as can fear that we might sabotage something in our remaining time. Always save a copy of a printed or email written notice, as the proof may be useful. BCC yourself, such as your personal email address, when sending a resignation letter.

Prior to giving notice, it's wise to ask the new employer (if we have one) whether we can start earlier on the off chance that we're terminated after giving notice. We should also say we don't think that will happen, showing faith that everything is good. Showing fear might suggest that it's not good and lead them to wonder if we're hiding something about how our current job is going. Always try to sound casual and like it's not a big deal. Or we can take our chances and be unemployed for two weeks, and collect two weeks of typically meager unemployment benefits.

I have seldom heard a surprised reaction to the question when I've asked. We all know people get fired on giving notice. It's exactly why the following things occur:

1. No one admits they are looking for a new job to anyone at their current one
2. HR/Recruiters understand we cannot talk while at work and agree to another time
3. HR/Recruiters agree to schedule interviews before or after work, or at lunch time
4. Job boards let us be anonymous or hide our resume from our current employer

Don't be the one person who doesn't accept that it happens. Just sound like it's a "just in case" question. They get it. And it's possible that our new employer has fired people for giving two-weeks' notice.

Anecdote Time

My job at the Pentagon was a poor fit, so I found another employer, who dragged their feet on making me an offer. My employer found out and told me Monday that I was being fired, my last day to be Friday. On Tuesday I called the new employer and told him I thought my current manager might know and could fire me, and I was asking if I could come on board if that happened because otherwise, I had to look elsewhere. He assured me he would get me an offer if that happened. On Thursday, I called him back and said I had been right; I had just been fired, and Friday was my last day. He leaped into action and we did paperwork the next day. I started the new job the next workday.

CHAPTER SEVEN

Reasons Jobs End

There are circumstances that can lead to job loss when we aren't quitting or being fired. This chapter is by no means a comprehensive list, just a few options we may not have considered.

Contract Loss

While we may be an employee, our company may lose the contract that is funding our position. This is especially common in government contracting, and is discussed in that chapter in Part Three. This is more likely to affect those who are doing the work that pays the bills, ironically. For example, a software developer who is programming for the client no longer has work to do when the contract ends, and if another suitable project/contract doesn't exist. Executives and HR staff are on company "overhead" and are not charging their time to a contract to begin with. Therefore, when contracts are lost, their positions are typically unaffected. The reason is that contracts call for people with specific skill sets. With a programmer, for example, the employer may have no need of one; only a client did, and with that client gone, the company has no need of the programmer and terminates them.

Budget Cuts

Whether it's our employer or their client (especially governments!), budgets are often annual. Sometimes this means cuts are needed and our neck might be on the chopping block. It is always wise to learn when an annual budget is being decided so that we may have time to find another position. We can sometimes overhear that a budget cut is in the works, or that someone must defend a budget. This should give us concern.

We may have a sense that our position isn't particularly needed, such as if work is slow. If our career is project-based and all seems a little quiet about future work, it is time to get the resume updated and put out feelers. I once lost two jobs in a row over this and then, while interviewing for others, lost a position that was defunded before they gave me the intended offer; I was getting so good at losing jobs for budget cuts I lost one before I had it.

Offered Unacceptable Work Changes

When suitable work ends, the company may offer us work that is unacceptable. They may not realize this, depending on circumstances. They might think we're okay with a change from being a SharePoint Programmer to SharePoint Administrator, for example, even though this is a change of profession. Both are technical work, which can lead a manager to offer this with a straight face, and an employee to accept it, too. But it may be so off-target for our career that we will leave the company.

While rare, some managers have so little idea what we do that they do not realize they are offering us such a change. I once had a manager so clueless that I was a programmer that he tried to turn me into a technical writer, then an administrative assistant, and refused to give me programming work for a long time. Much of this resulted from the employer no longer having a suitable project for me, and I should have left.

People early in their careers may be open to a wide variety of specializations in something like technical work and therefore seek to broaden skills and welcome a change. By contrast, someone with several years of experience can realize that they are spreading themselves too thin and cannot be considered a sufficient expert in their field, but a jack-of-all-trades. Therefore, such a change is unacceptable, and we put our careers ahead of the employer by leaving.

We sometimes receive the bait-and-switch, whether or not this is on purpose. It means being told the job entails certain things only for us to arrive on our first day and learn it does not. The contract we were supposed to be on might have been canceled or put on hold. Someone may have changed their mind. The hiring manager might leave and we aren't really wanted by anyone else, or they don't care what we were told.

We may also be told we will work in a job location only to be forced to work somewhere that is awful, either because of a commute, the staff there, or the office environment. The latter can include places with serious temperature control problems, noise, lack of decent working spaces, or other factors that make us dislike it. We may not have agreed to this, but we don't have a choice if we are an employee. We have given the right to make such decisions to our employer and our only recourse is often leaving. We can try to request these elements change, but the answer is often no for one major reason—the company needs someone to do this, and their needs are more important to them than ours.

Much of this depends on what we do for a living. If our work is project-based, like software development, these are more common. Those who work in administration are arguably less likely to experience dramatic shifts in their job.

Anecdote Time

I was once told that I could have a 90-minute (if I was lucky!) commute each way and continue doing the highly sought-after technologies that I specialized in. Or I could stay local and learn a technology I had never heard of and which didn't use my skills. I took the third option and quit for a job which wouldn't ruin my career and had a reasonable commute. I had worked there for fourteen months without suitable work, so this figured in my decision (that was long enough to hope it worked out).

CHAPTER EIGHT

Termination

One problem we can run into is being terminated with little to no warning. This is true of all arrangements. Many states are an "at-will" zone where we can be terminated, or quit, without justification or notice—or recourse. There's an old joke that the difference between employment and contracting or consulting is that employment carries *the illusion of job security*. In reality, none of them have it. As an employee, we can assume we're there indefinitely and can be caught flat-footed if terminated, especially when this happens through no fault of ours (i.e., we didn't do something that might've led us to see it coming).

It would be nice to live in a world where we only leave because we quit. But there is firing, being laid off, and "let go." We all know what fired means, but I'm going to suggest it is a somewhat hostile action with attitude, immediacy, and overtones of punishment. Being laid off suggests we did nothing wrong, but the company doesn't need us anymore for whatever reason, and we are being given a polite send off. They may even sound sorry to see us go or give us severance.

But the ubiquitous "let go," as in, "You're being let go" can be seen as slang for being *politely* fired. We did nothing overtly wrong, so they can't say we're being fired, but there is tension. Maybe someone doesn't like us, resents us, or has some other attitude—or thinks that we do. And maybe they're right; that we could have a good reason for it is irrelevant. And we won't be asked why we have an attitude, *especially* if they sense there's a good reason. They just want us to slip away. How do we react to being "let go?" Since they're trying to avoid a scene and attitudes being aired, we play along. They're being professional, and we should, too.

Be aware that some people interchange "let go" with "laid-off" as if they mean the same thing, and this might be true to them. We can tell which is really happening by their demeanor and our sense of whether this job was going all wrong or right. Place more emphasis on this than the words used.

Another option is being told that we can quit or be fired. Always quit—that will be the official reason in our HR file. If a future/prospective employer is verifying our employment record, they can learn we quit, or that the employer fired us; which would you prefer? They will not learn (from the employer) that we were blackmailed into quitting, but they can see a gap in our employment history; in most cases, being forced to quit means not having another job lined up. We may need to explain. It is okay to admit that management told us we could quit or be fired. However, "fired" is a loaded word, so we may want to claim they said, "quit or be let go," using that more innocent "let go" phrase, as this implies no wrongdoing by us.

The "quit or be fired" move always looks bad for our former employer more than us because it is an awful stunt, so we get a little sympathy. It is important to only explain it if we're *asked to*. Some people won't ask. An explanation should be short, like two sentences. Use the truth but with a positive spin that sounds reasonable. The old employer already sounds unreasonable by comparison, which is one reason we don't have to say much.

Why do companies do this? It varies by state, but state unemployment offices have policies about whether we qualify for benefits, and the manner of our most recent termination is the single greatest factor. If we're fired, we often get no benefits. Same if we quit. But if we were told to quit or be fired, we may get benefits. The reason is that the employer is admitting that they do not have *cause* to terminate us. If they did, they would just do it.

In the U.S., employers must pay unemployment insurance to the state. If we're unemployed and it's their fault, their payments may rise. If it's our fault, we're unemployed (we quit or our conduct led us to be fired), then we'll be denied benefits and the employer's pay rate is unaffected. Think of it like auto insurance. If we have a car accident and it's our fault, our insurance premiums may rise, but if the accident was someone else's fault, theirs will. Employers likely hope we'll tell the unemployment office we quit and that's all.

It is our word versus theirs that this threat ever took place; few companies will put the threat in writing. But the state unemployment office will investigate. When we file our claim, we should indicate that this threat happened. Some states even have a "was told to quit or be fired" option on a fill-in-the-blank claim form we complete. That's how widespread the practice is.

The employer may contest it, and if so, the state may ask for employment records, like meeting notes where we were warned about the behavior that eventually got us fired (supposedly). The state may ask for proof of a written warning and a chance to change our unacceptable behavior. They want to see that our employer gave us a chance to improve. If these don't exist, the state, in all likelihood, will determine that the employer is lying, side with us, and give us unemployment benefits because the corporation forced us to leave under duress that was not our fault. I have experienced this. Twice in a row. And the unemployment office sided with me both times.

Even if this doesn't happen, not everyone is professional about our termination. They can smile obscenely while doing it, for example. They can make personal remarks that we aren't the "kind of person" they want working there rather than the more innocent sounding, "it's not a good fit." Sometimes this is thoughtlessness; other times, they genuinely want to insult us, they have done so behind our backs, and this is their chance to do it to our face and then we're gone. Keeping our professionalism can be difficult, and many will say it's worth it, but if this sort of thing is happening, we're never coming back anyway. Decide how you can come away feeling satisfied, like justice has been served, and say your peace in as professional a way as possible.

Anecdote Time

At one job, HR called me while I was working from home on a Wednesday and told me I was being fired for doing so without permission. Stunned, I replied that I had worked from home every Wednesday for nearly six months, just like the rest of my team. She replied that someone had expected me to be there that day, which I had only just learned minutes earlier. Then she threw out two more excuses. In another violation of company policy, I had left my laptop on my desk the day before instead of locking it. While this was true, I had left for an offsite meeting, and then a manager forced me into a second, long, unexpected meeting so that I could not return to work and put it away because I had to get him to relieve the nanny and take care of my son.

And lastly, I had previously called into a different meeting instead of attending in person and was told that this meant I was indifferent to the meeting's content, the company's goals, a bad influence on my peers (who needed to be protected from me), and I was a threat to their business and needed to be immediately terminated. Talk about laying it on thick. In a "coincidence," the project I was on had been completed two days earlier. The same HR woman who did this knew I was going through an awful divorce while my wife was pregnant—and she did it anyway. When I pointed this out, she at least sounded genuinely aghast at what she was doing (I'm guessing she forgot). There is seldom much we can do when broadsided by unscrupulous employers.

CHAPTER NINE

When the Job is Ending

Once everyone knows we're leaving, life changes at work—unless we were unceremoniously shown the door. For those experiencing the usual two weeks, or a longer or shorter duration, there are factors to consider.

Asking for a Reference

References are valuable because some potential employers require them before even interviewing us, or after that and before a final hiring decision. Recent endorsements are better. If we change jobs every two or more years, it is more important to get references from each. This doesn't have to wait until we are leaving, but asking for a recommendation when we are not planning to go will make some assume we are looking, and this can actually get us fired. Be careful with this. If someone else is the one leaving, this is a great time to either offer to be a reference or ask them to be, as the assumption is that we may never hear from them again if we don't get their contact info now.

However, LinkedIn provides another way to reach out to former coworkers, even long after we have stopped knowing them. This is a good reason to connect with people, if still working with them or not. It has a fringe benefit of seeing what they are up to down the road, what job changes, promotions, or articles they have posted.

Naturally, we should ask those we think will agree. This can be coworkers, but managers are the best, particularly *our* manager. Next up would be their supervisor, such as a Vice President. It is best if we have actually interacted with that individual in a professional capacity, not just seen them at a work party. If we do client work, we can consider asking clients for a reference as well. For example, we might work for a private company that has a government contract, meaning we work with government staff much of the week, and even staff from other contractors. Any of these can be a reference.

It's better to ask when we're already open about our departure. If the company has let us go, this is easy because it's not a secret. If we have already found another job and given two weeks' notice, we are also in the clear. The problem is that a new employer probably wants to check the references before making us an offer, but we shouldn't ask for references at our current job until after we have the offer and have given notice. So how do we get around this?

This is a bigger problem at the start of our career when we are leaving our first corporate job, but we have likely had other jobs before this one, and we should use them as references. If we've only had one job before, working in a restaurant or as a babysitter, for example, we likely used them as a reference to get our first corporate job. Now we use them to get a *second* corporate job. Our new employer will understand if we can't give a reference from our current job. Once we get that second corporate job, we give our two weeks' notice. Then we ask people at our *first* corporate job to be a reference for later. Keep this pattern.

Some government agencies have policies forbidding staff from being a reference for us. We probably don't know if this is true and I've only learned it when the person I asked explained that such a policy existed. He was a peer, not my manager, and could do it, but if I had asked my manager at that government agency, she would've had to tell me no. Some will do it anyway.

Asking in person is best done if we're sure they will say yes. If we aren't sure, use email, which does not put them on the spot. But it also means being unable to judge the reaction until they respond, if they do. We can decide no reply means "no," or follow up, though this can be awkward. It can be best to talk to them face-to-face about anything other than our request, maybe mentioning our departure, and see if they raise the issue. If not, then ask, this time in person, if you feel comfortable.

Two weeks' notice that we are leaving is the standard. Those ten business days give our employer time to get a handover of our work to someone else. We can finish up what we're working on or bring it to a good stopping point. It gives them time to find a replacement, though it is unlikely anyone will start that soon. For us, we also benefit from closing out some work, which presumably matters to us. We have a chance to say goodbye to peers, ask for references, and prepare to transition. But it is still optional, even if the employee handbook says it is mandatory and talks about monetary fines they will enact if we don't. In many jurisdictions, those are not enforceable and even if they were, it is a bad look for the employer. Consult an attorney if truly concerned, but in the United-States, at-will employment means either party can terminate the relationship without warning; this implies without penalty, too. Some states have additional requirements, such as employers needing to pay all accrued paid-time off within 72 hours, for example.

We can give notice verbally, but we should still follow up with a quick email for posterity. HR will want this so that no one can tell them we quit when we didn't. A good time to give notice is closer to the workday's end, especially if only doing it in writing. The reason is that, if we give it earlier, such as first thing in the morning, we will wait for the reaction, and it may be a long time if our manager is busy or has many meetings. This can feel weird if six hours have gone by without an acknowledgement. Give notice an hour before leaving. Our manager knows when we go and will make time to respond or we will get a response early the next day. If there is tension between us and management, or we don't want to talk about it, doing it in writing creates distance. Verbal resignations are better if we have a good relationship with them.

The Final Two Weeks

Whether we resign, are laid off, or are "let go," life at work changes during the time in between management knowing we're leaving and our last day.

We cannot assume word will spread. Sometimes HR sends an announcement. Other times, no one says a word so that coworkers on our team don't even know it's our last day when they've had two weeks to learn this. Sometimes other staff appear to vanish and we inquire about their whereabouts only to learn from peers that they resigned, did the final two weeks after giving notice, and we never knew until weeks after their last day (I once assumed someone was on vacation precisely because no one said a word). Sometimes there's no announcement because the decision wasn't theirs and they are about to be unemployed, so a statement could seem inappropriate. If we are not liked or a performance review caused it, it may be better for us that few know.

We may be the only one telling others we're leaving. Be prepared with a positive-sounding answer about why. Leave behind any resentment. We can get away with a negative remark if it is something like the commute, because we aren't criticizing the company. But if we're talking to a confidant who already knows any negativity we feel about our job, then we can be honest if others can't overhear.

What are some positive things we can say? If we're changing technologies, for those who work in such things, this is a great excuse. Even if not, we can say that we're really looking forward to trying something new. Or that an opening came up, and we had to take it. A new job may allow us an opportunity, such as creating new software instead of maintaining old software, or launching a rebranding effort for a new employer if we are in marketing.

Many will ask us where we are going next. If "the unemployment line" is the answer, this is one reason not to tell anyone we are leaving; this doesn't feel great. Otherwise, admit the new company you'll be working for. Most will not ask many follow-up questions, but we may have a long conversation because some people are essentially saying farewell at the moment they learn we're going. If we tell them when we have a week left, don't expect another conversation on the last day. No one enjoys saying goodbye twice.

As for the job itself, the company will usually ask us to wrap up anything that we're doing and turn it over to others. This may involve training them on tasks that will be incomplete. Handle these gracefully, even if being forced out. It is expected and professional. We need to at least look like we *tried* to help the transition and mostly did a good job. Sometimes this transition happens so quickly that we really have nothing to do for nearly the entire two weeks. Enjoy it.

If there are local eateries or other establishments that you won't be enjoying for a long time, or ever, go one last time. Some coworkers may take us out for a meal or drink. Assume you are paying your own way but be gracious and thankful if anyone picks up your tab. Don't expect any of this to happen, however. Many jobs end with a whimper, especially if we're a consultant or contractor, and if there is high turnover, or what we do is project-based and people half expect some staff to not remain around for long. It certainly happens if we work alone a lot, and if we're the only one who does what we do.

We should take any files that we are legally allowed to. For example, the browser bookmarks that are career-related but not about that job. We should also download any digital copies of pay stubs if the company will end access by our last day. All companies will say that we cannot take other files such as documentation or software code we have written. But taking examples of some work we did is something may people do because we can leverage that at a new job.

Purists will object over this, but consider that people like coders often have a growing library of code we bring with them from one job to the next; this means the employer benefitted from that when we started. We have added to our library during our time with them and are walking out the door with those additions and changes. The person who replaces us is likely bringing yet another library of code developed at previous employers, once again benefitting the company. Legally, this argument won't hold up, but some justify it in their heads. They may be right.

Exit Interviews

The company sometimes asks us to do an exit interview with HR. While they may set aside thirty minutes to do it, it is often far less, especially if we're tightlipped. We may refuse, but this can look bad and there is a better way of handling it—do it and say only positive things. Even if we have a gripe, we must aim for constructive criticism or say nothing. And don't show an attitude! This is the best approach anyway. Just as first impressions matter, final ones do, too, and airing grievances on the way out the door is not wise, even if we are never returning.

We can tell ourselves that we are doing the company a favor with the truth, a last chance to improve, and we may genuinely want to help, but many businesses will not change. This is one reason the exit interview is uncommon. The process can suggest that employers do care, and maybe they do, but they are still unlikely to make changes for at least two reasons: there is less interest in what a soon-to-be former employee thinks, and changes can be hard to implement, depending on what they are.

Even if they call the meeting something other than an "exit interview," the word "interview" is a sign of how we should treat this—just like the hiring interview. This is the attitude to have. Be positive. Smile. Find a good spin to put on everything and talk more about a promising future than about a negative past (that would be them). We don't want to lay it on too thick about how great our next employer will be, but it is standard practice to say something like, "I'm excited by another opportunity" and then follow that up with some innocent reasons.

It is fair to admit we did not think working there would lead to where we want to be, as our departure already implies this. Some excuses are better than others, like the commute or even teleworking options and general work-life balance. And of course, the prospects of future work, which is fine to mention if work is drying up where we are now—we might do them a favor by leaving before they tell us to quit or be fired. We can mention salary as well, but this opens the door to a counteroffer that can make this awkward if we just want to leave and are not admitting we hate our job.

While companies may honestly want to fix problems so they retain other staff better, the case can be made that the problems leading to our departure are not ours to fix and are not our responsibility to bring to light, especially now that we're leaving. Employers won't like that idea (we aren't going to say it), but they may understand if we believe the truth is not in our best interests and that we may be reluctant. Hopefully they foster an exit interview mood that is sincere enough to inspire our confidence that we can be more honest. But tread lightly here. It is possible to ruin our chances of ever returning, should we want to, by what we say on the way out.

The Last Day

If we're leaving without tension, the last day at work can be as easy as the first day. In both cases, they don't expect us to do any actual work, usually, though this depends on our position. Many assume we just don't care because we won't be there to deal with any work we do poorly once it is discovered (after we leave), and this plays a role in everyone's attitude. The day is often pointless and mostly a chance to complete emptying our desk, taking things to the car, submitting final timesheets, turning in our badge, and other housekeeping. We can do this in less than an hour, and yet we may have seven more to go.

Partly for this reason, employers, or at least our manager, are often fine with this being a half day but paying us for the whole thing. They may suggest we leave early. Or they may ask what time we're leaving, implying it can be long before eight hours is up. Take the offer, be casual about it, and do it. But we should expect to be there all day and alternate between closing out, chit chat, and wasting time on the internet.

If we're new to the corporate world, we might think our last day is special and people will line up to say goodbye. This isn't true (unless we are unusually popular or we're a manager and people are *still* sucking up). For everyone else, it's just another day, and the next workday is, too, and we stopped mattering because we won't be there. This viewpoint starts *before* our last day, almost as soon as word gets out that we're leaving. One reason we can leave early without complaint is that we've probably said all of our goodbyes... and yet we're still there. The "Yeah, just go already" sentiment can hang in the air. Don't take it personally.

As we are actually heading for the door, refrain from a last round of goodbyes. They're busy doing their job. Some will give heartfelt farewells, but the reaction from others can range from an unspoken, "Didn't we already say goodbye?" to "What are you still doing here?" If we're going to do that, avoid the impression of wanting people to express, one more time, that they are sad to see us go. Tell your manager "this is it" and leave, saying "take care" or whatever to anyone you pass along the way to the door.

CHAPTER TEN

After Leaving

Before we leave the job, many will say they want to stay in touch. This sentiment often dies shortly after we go. Some were just being nice. Others meant it. But the result is the same. Leaving is an act of moving on. The job is part of our past. Even if we return to being staff, that will be a new future. And while it may have a connection to the past, or a resumption of it, these are two separate lives right now. That future is "vapor ware"—it doesn't exist. And to those we have left behind, we don't exist anymore because we aren't around. We are outside that ecosystem, and they are outside ours. This is a major reason why leaving can be awkward. We might be implicitly rejecting the employer from now on, but we're also doing it to everyone working there.

The exception is anyone we have become good friends with, but there is a difference between work friends and "unqualified" friends. The latter are people we are pals with regardless of circumstance. Work friends are only such because we work together, and now that we don't, we aren't. Not really. It depends on our definition, but, unless we have spent time outside of work with people, we will not interact much again. "Outside of work" does not include happy hours or the company softball team, as those are still associated with the job. But if we're fortunate and desire it, we may continue happy hours if we're still nearby. Otherwise, move on.

Staying in touch is still an option, and several ways of doing it have their considerations. Connecting on LinkedIn is great for commenting on their activities there and vice versa. As long as we don't behave badly, for example, this is almost the optimal way to remain connected. What we always want is a positive reaction to interaction, and this is one that can produce a fond "happy to see you" feeling even if they say nothing.

At the other extreme is physically stopping in at a former employer without warning or invitation. Don't do this. Most times, we don't have a badge to get past the entrance, so we won't get far anyway, but that depends on how recently we left. Come by soon enough and someone may recognize us and think we still work there, holding the door for us as we piggyback our way in. But technically, they can consider us a security violation. Being tackled and taken away for interrogation is unlikely (I think), but we won't get a positive reaction, even from people who like us. A scowl of confusion and "What are *you* doing here?" are more likely, before they realize their tone is off-putting and try to soften it, if they bother to. It really is like we have left a club or clique and are not members anymore. We are not welcome. We don't belong there.

Sending the occasional email is okay, but if all we're doing is trying to stay in touch, don't expect a response unless you were besties. It is better to have a reason, like a question, or if they have agreed to be a reference, and we're still using them that way, to reach out and catch up and ask if it's still okay. And don't expect anyone to email you first to find out how your "I moved on from you" life is going. All of this is true with calls and voicemails as well, but calls can be considered more intrusive. Strive to stay in touch in small bits when you have something worthwhile to say. Posting our own content on LinkedIn is great for making others want to reach out to *us*.

We can rate the employer on websites that allow this. If we have anything negative to say, it is best to wait at least six months and be generic in our description to avoid them identifying us, even though our review is anonymous. We should also try to lose any poor attitudes we may have gained because of this job. A poor experience can make us cynical in ways that impact our attitude and performance from now on, giving a past job too much influence on our present and future prospects.

Focus on your future.

Anecdote Time

After six months at my first corporate job, they eliminated my position because of funding, and I began working for another group one floor down. I sometimes dropped by my former team, but they always assumed I wanted something. On learning I just came by to say hello, they looked at me in disbelief. Not sure what to make of it and feeling unwelcome, I slowly stopped doing it.

At another job, I became friendly with a woman who invited me and my wife to her wedding (we went). We friended each other on Facebook, which was new then (LinkedIn did not exist). We once talked about how former coworkers act like you're dead (i.e., ghost you) if you leave, and she aired her exasperation about it. Before long, I left the company. Imagine my surprise when she did that very thing to me.

Part Three

The Basics

CHAPTER ELEVEN

Employment Types

M ost of us are going to be an employee somewhere, but there are other types of gigs. What follows is a high-level explanation of pros and cons to each and some things to watch out for.

Contracting

There are two types of contracting: 1099 and contract-to-hire.

Independent Contracting (1099)

Colloquially called 1099 in the U.S., this contracting option is nicknamed for the IRS form that such individuals must file for taxes. We are not an employee of any kind. This is the easiest arrangement due to the lack of paperwork. The company that hires us pays gross wages, meaning they take no money out for taxes or anything else. We have no insurance benefits, either, whether work health, retirement, or even holiday or vacation pay. There's nothing. Just the whole paycheck and no frills.

Most companies pay weekly and don't require an invoice from us. We can fill out a direct deposit form or have a check sent to us and it's all straightforward and lacking encumbrance. Or at least, at the time. We're responsible for paying taxes ourselves, and this can be challenging.

Contract-to-Hire

Contract-to-hire means we won't be an employee... yet. We will be a contractor for usually three to six months. This period allows the company an extended evaluation of us to see if we're a good fit. It also allows *us* to see if the job is a good fit. Often, that employer will have hired a recruiting company to find and retain us as the latter's employee for this duration. At the contract's conclusion, if we still want to become an employee and they still want us, we join the other firm. For example, XYZ Firm hires 123 Recruiters, who hire us as a 123 Recruiters employee for six months, and at the conclusion of this, we become XYZ Firm's employee.

We are usually paid by the hour and have reduced or no benefits; a day off can mean doing so without pay. As a result, we may ask for a higher hourly rate to compensate for this and having to pay for items like health insurance on our own, as two examples.

If we don't feel the job is a good fit, all we need to do is look for another job with enough time that we don't end up unemployed when the contract ends. We can be honest and tell the recruiting firm that we don't think it's right for us, even why. If we have done well, they will still think of us favorably and offer to find us other positions. We should accept that offer but continue our own search.

But sometimes the XYZ Firm doesn't want to bring us on. This can be our performance or changing circumstances, such as contract loss. In the latter case, they may appreciate our work and try to find us other employment with them, just in a different position. This can sometimes result in a poor match, in which case it is often better to move on. Be graceful and leave with good references.

If we want to be XYZ Firm's employee and they want us, too, we must do the same sort of paperwork we'd normally do regarding an offer letter and employment application. It's important to know that whatever hourly rate the recruiting firm offered us might be the same one we're offered now, when it is converted to a yearly salary. However, they may also decide it was inflated and reduce the salary offer accordingly. It can be an unpleasant surprise, which is why we must negotiate the salary long before now, when the recruiting company first contacts us and wants an hourly rate *and* the later salary. Better firms will require this, but we should ask if they do not.

As our contracting time ends, companies can be casual about what comes next, not advising us whether or not we'll be coming on board. We should ask the recruiting firm at least a month in advance, but they often can't get an answer either. It is incumbent on them to do this. If we're not getting details, it is usually the other company failing to provide them. This is a bad sign about mismanagement and our prospects there.

If they bring us on, this may result in us working an additional few weeks or a month through the recruiting firm while they approve paperwork. This is seamless. But if they don't intend to hire, they can leave us hanging. Companies can tell us they will hire us and then not produce any paperwork or offer, and say we aren't being hired after all with only days of the contract left. Suddenly we're out of a job, with no recourse and only a useless apology from the recruiting firm. It's hard to tell what happened and if they lied to us.

Being an Employee

Being an employee has several advantages if it is full time (usually 40+ hours per week). This includes literal benefits like vacation pay and several types of insurance, both of which are costly to go without. We can contribute to a retirement plan and have matching monetary contributions from the employer, and these can become significant if we remain with the company long enough. None of those apply to contractors or consultants.

We may also be treated differently and arguably better. The rationale is that we are supposedly permanent staff and investing in the company's goals and mission and intending to rise through the ranks into management and beyond. This happens, but for most staff, we will leave long before then. How are we treated better? We are included when others may not be, whether this is information or actual events. We are "first class" citizens by comparison, and there can be a subtle—or not-so-subtle—difference in how people interact with us. Employees are welcomed warmly, while contractors and consultants can be treated like the copier repair man—a temporary person whom there is no point getting to know.

But there are disadvantages, too. Being taken for granted is among them. This can manifest as little thought given to how we feel about changes. If we have career goals, the company sees those as less important than theirs, which is not surprising. In their view, we are there to help them realize their goals, not ours. What all parties want is for these to align, and they should when we start and agree to partner, but they almost always diverge, eventually.

When we are job hunting, employers woo us with a variety of items: salary, benefits, work location, job duties, and potentially the project if our work is project-based. At this stage, we are choosing these, but once we become an employee, we lose all control. Our employer can change any of these without warning or justification, and we must either accept or quit.

We can ask for and usually get a meeting with our manager to discuss a change, but we will usually be told that this is what the company needs us to do. Notice how the focus is on their needs, not ours. Our manager may understand, and this decision is often not theirs but someone above them, so while they will "get it," their hands are tied. We must not come on too strong with our unhappiness because we may convince them that we will quit. If we're thinking we want them to sense this, because they will then realize they will lose a valued employee, we should rethink that. They won't bend to our will and forget about this unwanted job change. But they may decide we are not a "team player," and no longer a good fit for the company, and possibly let us go.

If the work we do is project-based, or for company clients, such as with software development that seldom lasts indefinitely, the projects can change unexpectedly and involve a location change that might adversely affect our life. If we work in technology, we may need to use ones we have no interest or experience in, while also no longer working on ones we want to keep current on. Sometimes these details even change between the day we are hired and our first day of employment. This is usually by accident, but sometimes it is on purpose, a ploy known as the "bait and switch." They think we won't quit because of it, since we just started, and two job changes in quick succession looks bad, but it actually doesn't if we explain to later employers what happened (making it sound like an accident, not a nefarious plot). This sort of thing is seldom if ever done to us as contractors and consultants because we control all of this and arguably have one foot out the door all the time already.

Anecdote Time

Early in my career, several employers noticed my writing skills and repeatedly made me do documentation instead of programming, not in addition to it (there's a difference). One tried to turn me into a technical writer, a lower paying profession. Sometimes a skill is almost used against us this way. A similar version can happen with technology—several employers hired me to do advanced programming, but then they won contracts for less advanced ones and forced me to do them because I had those listed on my resume earlier in my career. I solved both issues by reducing or removing mention of these skills from my resume.

Consulting

Consulting typically means we own a company, possibly as an LLC, for example, where we are the only staff. Our business is registered with the state and may have a website, business cards, letterhead, an email domain (randy@myllc.com), and several kinds of insurance (liability, errors and omissions). They pay us gross wages and we must pay quarterly (and yearly) taxes based on estimates that we either do personally or have our CPA calculate. When a client hires us, it is via a corp-to-corp (C2C) agreement that is like an employment contract. They may ask us to submit proof our business is in current standing (sometimes known as Articles of Organization from the state) and proof of insurance. Setting up an LLC is outside the scope of this book, but much of what happens once we start the job is like contracting.

As an LLC, we can get ourselves benefits like short-term disability and life insurance that is associated with our company. We can do retirement accounts and health insurance this way, but it depends on what country we live in and other details that interested workers need to research if interested. We can replicate many of the employer-supplied benefits we would have access to as an employee. Forming a company and working through it also protects us from liability issues; our LLC can be sued, but we can't be; our personal assets are protected. This is not true for a contractor. We might view consulting as "contracting with a net."

An exception to this is money. Employees are paid every two weeks or bi-monthly. Contractors are often paid weekly. But a corporation? We must send an invoice for the last month and then wait between one and three months to be paid for an entire month's work at once. This can make this existence precarious without sufficient savings to carry us over. In theory, once we're established, this problem abates, but not always. We can be without a client for a while, then not be paid for even longer despite working. And in the United States, April is a double-whammy: we must pay quarterly taxes and, if our estimates for last year were off in the wrong direction, we might have to pay substantial past-year taxes. To make matters worse, the next quarterly tax payment is not three months later in July, but in June. And sometimes we just started a new client (we won't be paid for months) after a period without one (we also aren't being paid).

Determining our hourly rate can also be problematic for those new to corp-to-corp. This also lies outside the scope of this book, but we can charge substantially more because of our business costs. This doesn't mean we are raking in that much cash, though. We are compensating for costs and failing to do this would mean earning far less money.

As we would expect, companies are formal about bringing us on as employees and consultants. They are also formal with termination of employees. But they are seldom official about terminating consultants. They can be downright cavalier about ending our time with them, telling us the same day that we're gone in under two hours despite weeks being left on the contract. Contracts are often for durations lasting months, and when the contract is ending, but the work is not, or we have earned apparent respect, they may talk about extending us. And yet they will often not do another contract, or waffle, or change their mind at the last minute after effectively stringing us along. The result is suddenly having no client and our next one not lined up. This happened so often in my career that I expected it. We have to look out for ourselves, and this can mean finding our next client and leaving one that we like but which does not have its act together. I have politely reminded clients and still had them do this.

One advantage to consulting is that we do not have to admit to not having a client when looking for a new one, or even to switch to being an employee. Our client history is proprietary information. We technically still have a job, so we are not unemployed, even though we may have no income. But we do not have to divulge that or when our current client work ended.

Another advantage is that we can look for a job while we already have a client because the latter already knows we are temporary. They don't get upset about us looking to leave because this was implied all along. The lack of sneaking around is refreshing and feels very adult, compared to the fear that employees have of being fired for looking at other opportunities. We are also less likely to receive the "bait and switch" treatment, both because we are probably a specialist and because we always have one foot out the door anyway, and a client pulling this stunt might make us leave at once and they know it.

A disadvantage to consulting is that we are the first ones to be let go when trouble arises. If downsizing occurs, some employers can't justify keeping temporary staff (us) while laying off permanent ones, so we may disappear first. If a problem exists on the contract, such as someone making a mistake, they may blame and terminate us so that they can save face to their client and say it wasn't one of them, but an outsider (us).

Anecdote Time

I once received a negative one-week notice. My manager told me on Friday that there was a problem with the paperwork to extend my contract beyond its end that day. I was told not to come in on Monday, when he called me and told me to come in Tuesday, when he pushed me to Wednesday. This continued until Friday, when he told me it looked like I wasn't coming back. I had been out of work for a week before I knew it. If you're thinking this was some amateur company doing this, it was one of the biggest defense contractors in the world.

CHAPTER TWELVE

Government Contracting

This chapter is a high-level overview of government contracting and the issues that arise from working for government agency. We may work in an area, such as in or near Washington, D.C., where this is very common with the federal government, but all regions have state, county, and city or town governments.

Overview

Governments have two kinds of people performing the work: government employees and contractors. The former work directly for an agency, such as the State Department, NASA, state police, local health department, or county government, to name a few; we'll refer to these as agencies for this chapter. Everyone else works for a company and is considered a "contractor." There is a reason for this term.

Using NASA as an example, an agency is divided into smaller entities, the names of which change by the place. What they have in common is that we might work for NASA, for example, but we really work for the XYZ Division of Directorate 700 of NASA Goddard (one of their locations), which is part of NASA overall. When XYZ Division realizes that their government staff cannot perform the work for whatever reason (manpower), they create a contract. This is put out for companies to bid on, and they compete to win the contract. Each company submits a proposal that a responsible party in the government evaluates against other proposals, and they choose a winner.

These contracts are to administer something often called a "program," which is a body of work to be performed. As a result, there is a role of Program Manager. Someone from the agency does not fill this role. Rather, the Program Manager works for the company that won the contract. This person handles all the staff doing the work under that contract. We often work directly for and report to this person, who is typically at the agency site, but variation exists here. The Program Manager might mostly work there, we might while they don't, neither of us might, or both of us might work onsite. The Program Manager answers to two people: their own manager at their employer company, and the government person responsible for the contract's work. There are various terms for this person, and it varies by the agency, such as Contracting Officer's Representative (COR).

The contracts are almost always hourly rather than fixed price. The contract may call for ten people: the Program Manager, Project Manager, one technical writer, one graphic designer, one software architect, and five software developers, for example. Each of these will perform forty hours of work on the contract per week, except the Program Manager, who is probably overseeing multiple programs, often for the same agency such as NASA, but not necessarily. The Project Manager might also be split between projects. One aspect of this is that we usually won't be allowed to work over forty hours a week, and since most people don't want to work unpaid overtime, we needn't worry. If we want a flexible work schedule, our employer may allow this, but the agency may not.

A fixed price contract is different. This means the company will be paid a set amount of money to perform the work, regardless of how long it takes. A company can effectively save money by doing the work in less time, and the staff are then free to work on something else and earn the company more money. But if the project takes longer, the company is paying staff more money for more time that cannot be charged to another client.

Hourly contracts are the norm with the federal government and results in the "body in a seat" phenomenon. This means that for each hour we are charging time to the government contract, our company earns money. We might earn $50 an hour, but the going rate that the government pays could be above $100. Our employer is pocketing the difference. That is how they make money and pay for benefits, office space, equipment, the holiday party, and the staff who are not on contracts, like HR, proposal writers, and executives.

And us, when we are not on a contract. This is known as being on "overhead" and is a perilous place to be if we are supposed to be assigned to a contract. Being on overhead is deadly to our job for one simple reason—we are costing the company money, not earning it for them. Any loyalty to us, if it existed, stops here.

As for being a "body in a seat," this means it sort of doesn't matter if we're doing any work. Our employer makes money anyway. What matters is that they can charge our time for a contract. They may require us to write a weekly status report detailing what we did for the agency, and we should have things to do, but there is great flexibility here. Some jobs are almost openly "body in a seat" situations, between us and our manager, but of course we must keep up appearances to the government staff. When interviewing us, some companies will even say it is not a "body in a seat" job.

Sometimes our position turns into this sort of job for various reasons, like projects ending (successfully or not) but the contract continuing, or the slowing of work. This can create a somewhat relaxing environment where we are not expected to do much and there is therefore less stress, but it is a bad sign. Extricating ourselves from this is sometimes not possible while remaining with the company because *someone* is contractually required to be the body in that seat even if no longer needed.

Another problem is that, when the contract inevitably ends, our employer may not have another contract to which they can assign us. Very often, those contracts have already started and are fully staffed. Or we can be assigned, but any of several problems can arise. The commute to the new agency might be awful. The technology might be a dead-end or horribly dated. The project can be an utter mess. The new team we work with might not be a good fit. It might be a dreaded office environment like the open floor plan. The work might not align with what we do for a living, such as being forced to be a SharePoint administrator instead of a SharePoint developer, or write documentation for the next year because we're an excellent writer.

A contract ending is cause for worry, and we should always be subtly asking management about other work the company does, not like we're trying to switch, but just to find out what else is out there. Being proactive might save us from the chopping block if the company is thinking to end our employment because they don't need us anymore. If we have asked about the company's other efforts and have done well on our current contract, we might be pulled from one to another. Sometimes this happens when we don't want it to, such as a new contract being awarded and our skill set is deemed appropriate, so they switch us. We have no say in this, typically.

When they hire us, our employer may want us to redo our resume in their format. The reason is that, when the proposal team is assembling the proposal, they will include our resume and that of other staff members to prove the existing talent is on staff and qualified. If they win the contract, the agency may expect us to be assigned to it. We may never know that our resume is being used to solicit one contract or another until told of our assignment switch, but we will have a general sense when we are asked to reformat it. If it seems like we are being used, it's because we are.

This has one advantage, however. Some contracts require staff with qualifications who have specific certifications. If we hold one or more, potential employers can be more interested in us precisely because our employment lets them use us to bid on contracts that they might otherwise be unable to compete for. We won't see a kickback for "helping" with this, but it may figure in our salary as an unspoken reason we command the one we do. In a variation on this, some firms want to become a Microsoft Partner, and among the requirements to become one, the company must have several staff with specific certifications. Employers want this for several reasons, one of which is that some agencies stipulate that only Microsoft Partners can submit proposals for some contracts.

Contracts are awarded for a period of years with "option" years. This means a five-year contract has four. Toward the end of each year, the agency has the option to end the contract if the contractor isn't performing up to expectations. If we are being hired for a contract, we will often be told, "we're starting the first year of a five-year contract with option years." Then we will get some reassurance from the recruiter that the company has a great relationship with the agency and no issues are expected. Take this with a grain of salt, but it isn't common for contracts to be lost because this means a Program Manager may lose their job, costing many others theirs, losing a lucrative contract for their employer, and risking the company ever winning another contract with that agency. This is a big deal.

But companies lose contracts for no other reason than that it ends. The work usually continues, but the proposal, bidding, and award process starts over, and the same company may not win it again. Many factors contribute to this, including being underbid. If our company loses, that means most of the existing staff that the agency is familiar with are about to vanish, taking institutional knowledge with them and requiring a transfer of knowledge that is seldom optimal. The agency wants continuity, which means those people remaining on the job despite their employer being booted. How can the agency have its cake and eat it, too?

By the new company hiring many of our employer's staff, including us. This happens often. Our current employer will not resist it because they want to make the agency happy in hopes of winning future contracts. The result is that, with our manager's blessing, the contract-winning firm may invite us to a meeting with a representative (probably the new Program Manager or a Director/VP) to discuss a job offer. This can be like an informal job interview. We aren't really being interviewed for a job we already have, but hearing what they are offering, learning about their company, and discussing whether there is a path forward for us to remain. They already want us or we wouldn't be having this conversation. Our employer may have given them our resume, and they may ask for an updated one from us. This meeting will usually involve the discussion of compensation and their benefits. It is a negotiation.

We should not be afraid to ask for more. We may be due an annual raise so that accepting the same salary costs us money. They may have a standard two-week vacation offer but we have three-weeks already, so we admit this and ask if they can do it. They will either say yes or they think so, then get back to us later. For retirement accounts and "vesting," their hands can be tied. I cover this in a subsequent chapter, but when we contribute to retirement accounts, companies match, but the amount of their contributions that we keep depends on how long we have been employed. It can be something like another 20% for each year. If we are three years in, we are at 60% and will miss out on the remaining 40% if we leave (plus the 100% every year thereafter). This is something to consider, but our new employer usually cannot do anything about this, meaning we will not start with them at that 60% tier. We are starting over. They understand this, and it can be one reason to ask for a higher salary and get it. Try to look at contract loss as an opportunity, and don't be afraid to remain with the current employer if everything is good, but we must first seriously consider our prospects at both.

Security Clearances

Some positions require us to have a security clearance. If we don't have one, an employer may not consider us as a candidate, but they may be willing to "sponsor" us to get one. They will pay the cost. All we need to do is fill out an extensive application our employer will provide to us. Once we turn it in, the government agency will investigate us and decide whether to grant us the clearance.

While this is occurring, we can sometimes start the job with the caveat that if they do not give the clearance, they will let us go. Other companies may tell us we cannot start until the clearance is granted. The problem is that the process takes months, so we should have employment in the meantime. They may grant us an interim clearance in a few weeks, with this allowing us to get started. This varies, so we must ask HR as we are discussing possible employment.

Note that it is not possible to sponsor yourself for a clearance, even if you have a business, as consultants do.

Once we have a clearance, a company must "hold it." This means they must associate it with them. If we leave the company, and our next position also requires and can use the clearance, our new employer should start the transfer to them. However, they do not always follow through on this even if we ask and they confirm they did it. Unfortunately, we must take their word for it, but most take care of it. If we no longer need our clearance, it will remain "active" for two years. After that, it becomes "inactive." This means that if we need it again, it is relatively easy, inexpensive, and quick for an employer to request it to be reactivated.

Clearances do not last forever. They must be periodically renewed. This means being investigated all over again. This is one reason to save a copy of our responses to the application so that we do not have to gather the information once more. The period before renewal depends on the clearance but is typically five years or more. If we are in this five-year period and the clearance becomes inactive, this is when it can be reactivated. If the five years have passed, the clearance is effectively gone, and we start over. This may happen even if the clearance is still active. It is our employer's responsibility to maintain this, but they sometimes fail to do so.

Our employer has a "security officer" in charge of this. This doesn't mean an armed person standing guard. It means someone trained in the maintenance and processing of clearances for an employer, for whom he or she works. This will be the one who points us to the application and monitors its progress once electronically submitted to the evaluating agency. We bring our questions about the process and status to this person. By law, they cannot share the details of our information with anyone at the company, including human resources, except for the investigation's result: getting a clearance or not.

There are many details to gaining and keeping a clearance that lie outside the scope of this book, as our focus is on issues that can arise during this process. But unless we have serious wrongdoing in our past, we can usually obtain one. Even if we have misbehaved and there is a record of it, being honest can earn us a clearance. Any deceit disqualifies us. They may interview families and past or present neighbors. And they will certainly interview us. Who investigates varies, but the FBI are common investigators, so we may have the chance to meet an FBI agent.

If we have an active clearance, it may surprise us to learn that it is not valid everywhere. Many agencies require their own clearances. This means we could get a Department of Defense (DOD) clearance and be able to work for the Army, Navy, etc., but then Customs and Border Protection (CBP) won't accept that and wants to investigate all over again to grant *their* clearance. The result is having multiple clearances.

Another issue that can arise is having the wrong level clearance. We may have a Secret but need a Top Secret. This means being declined for the position or doing another clearance. We might also have the reverse situation. In this case, we should ask during the interview phase if the employer can hold the higher clearance, even though they don't need us to have it. The answer varies, but in my experience the answer is typically yes. There is a reason. The employer's security "office" is certified and trained up to a certain level and if they go high enough, they can hold the higher clearance. If they aren't, they can't.

A security clearance is valuable and can earn us over five figures higher per year. But if we lose it, this does not necessarily mean our salary goes down.

At www.clearancejobs.com/security-clearance-faqs, you can learn more.

Anecdote Time

I once had an active Top Secret DOD clearance and started a new job with CBP, who wanted to do their own investigation while I started the job. This should have progressed through three stages: starting without the clearance, being given an interim one, and then getting the final clearance. Two months into it, they introduced me to a new guy who had the same skills as me. This came as a surprise. My manager asked me to teach him how my system worked, with me wondering why.

Within a week, and a day or two after Christmas, I was "let go" effective immediately. CBP told me I didn't even make it to the interim stage; they had denied my clearance. The CBP agency rep was shocked and said she had never seen that before, given my TS. She couldn't tell me why it happened but said I could request my clearance file, so I did and found nothing. They admitted to having known for a week and getting me to train my replacement while lying to me about it. They had also wanted to be nice and not fire me right before Christmas.

Years earlier, Company 1 held my clearance, but I quit for Company 2, who said they would hold it. Then I quit for Company 3, who also said they would hold it. Then I told Company 4 that I had an active Secret clearance and came to interview. On my way out, the recruiter told me there was a problem with my clearance. I called Company

3, who confirmed they had never transferred it. I had worked there for about twelve months, not twenty-four, so I thought it should still be active at Company 2, but when I called them, they confirmed they had never transferred it either during the fourteen months there. My clearance had gone inactive. When I confirmed this to Company 4, they still brought me on and sponsored me for a Top Secret clearance (an upgrade!), but they dropped my salary offer by $7000. You win some, you lose some. With TS clearance in hand, I left six months later... for more money.

CHAPTER THIRTEEN

Benefits

Employers offer a package of benefits to employees, the details of which vary by the company. We will touch on some highlights and issues that can arise.

One is that we cannot change our enrollments in benefits whenever we want, with the possible exception of retirement accounts. We can choose when hired, at the annual reselection period, or when we have a "qualifying life event." This usually means a change in family (our child is born) or our spouse's job changes. HR will provide a list of these events.

Employers supply several types of insurance: health, dental, vision, life, short- and long-term disability, and AD&D. There are few problems that arise, but once we make our selections, it is wise to write them down. The reason is that we need to renew the choices every year. Sometimes this is as simple as checking all the same pre-filled boxes on an online form, where our previous choices are already selected, but it usually isn't. Since most of us forget exactly what we chose, we have to go through figuring out what we want (or what we already have) over again... unless we wrote it down or took screen shots. This also happens when changing jobs or when our employer changes their offerings.

Leave

There are multiple kinds of leave, and while some are expected, others may not exist.

Vacation

The standard found everywhere is vacation leave. This won't be available to 1099 contractors or consultants, only employees. At least two weeks is standard in the United States, but three weeks is common for older employees, and those with long tenure can gain even more. A common practice is to gain additional hours with every year of employment. This figure is negotiable, especially for more seasoned staff, who may be used to three weeks but be changing to an employer who is only offering two for all new employees. We can request the extra hours and often receive them.

The balance is usually accrued, meaning that in our first pay period, we have zero hours. The accrual is by pay period and will be a figure like 5.5 hours. We can therefore estimate how many hours we expect to have by an intended vacation. Multiply the hours per pay period by the number of pay periods.

An employer may allow us to go negative on our balance. For example, we need 40 hours but only have 32, going -8. If they allow this, it is always on a case-by-case basis, with a reminder not to make a habit of it. The amount we intend to go negative affects their willingness, naturally. It also depends on circumstances. If we had a vacation planned before starting the job, and the vacation occurs within three months, we may not have enough hours. We should mention this during the last stages of hiring, when we have already passed the interview and are in final negotiations to come on board. Being upfront about this makes agreement much more likely. They understand that when we booked our vacation, we could not have known for sure we would change employers even if we had been looking. If our balance is still negative when we leave the company, they will take money out of our last paycheck.

Another option is to take the time off without pay. If our previous employer paid out our vacation balance when we left, we may have the money for it anyway. Then we don't need to go negative on our balance, or maybe not as much. Consider your options and ask your manager or HR.

If we have a positive balance when leaving a company, they usually pay this out to us in our final paycheck, but not always. The best time to find out is during our orientation with HR, when the question sounds innocent. Asking after this can sound like we are thinking to quit. Another option is to discreetly ask another staff member, on learning that they are leaving, if their vacation balance is being paid out.

When planning a vacation, we should float the idea past our manager before booking anything. This is a courtesy but also expected. They must approve our absence regardless of vacation hours being used or not. If they say no, we can't go without losing our job or getting into trouble. Managers and employers don't decline without a good reason, so just as they expect us to ask first, we expect them to say yes. But if the vacation is longer than ten working days, they may be more hesitant. It also depends on our profession and other circumstances. Float it first, do your planning, confirm it with your manager and officially submit a leave request, and then book the arrangements.

We can also use vacation for a single day, but some employers frown on, or even forbid, using an hour here or there. Learn the situation from HR. Some people try to call in sick, or claim an emergency, but this can backfire if our manager suggests we work from home instead. Doing this too many times also becomes suspicious. If we come back with a nice tan the next day from a golf or beach outing, it might be the last time we set foot in the building.

Sick

Some employers also have sick leave, which can only be used for medical appointments or days home. If we want five days off for the beach and only have four days of vacation (32 hours), we can't use a day of sick leave for the remaining day. We can try, of course, and be denied. And we can claim when that day rolls around that we got sick, but this is likely to be viewed with suspicion. They might ask us to show a doctor's note proving it. We might even get away with it once.

While we can often use vacation leave in small increments of even less than one hour, some employers require sick leave being in blocks of four to eight hours. This is not ideal when we only need two for a doctor's appointment, so if we learn this is true, we may try to schedule some back-to-back.

Like vacation leave, sick leave is accrued per pay period and must usually be acquired before we can use it. We may be able to go negative. One problem with a separate sick leave is that this is in exchange for vacation hours. Instead of three weeks of vacation, we might have only two and one week of sick leave. On paper this seems fine until we consider the restrictions on sick leave.

It can tempt us to go into the office while sick to save our leave, but working from home makes this less necessary, if we are up for it. We must decide how we want to manage this, but our manager must approve unexpected working from home. Making us come in while sick is not something they can do, but if we're out of sick leave, we must either use vacation hours or take leave without pay, the latter requiring HR approval. For this reason, we may want to avoid involving them any more than necessary.

Jury Duty

Some employers have jury duty leave for up to three consecutive working days. We may have to prove, with documentation supplied by the court, that we were required for that long. This is straightforward and without issue unless they choose us for a longer trial. Unlike other kinds of leave, this is not usually accrued but available from day one.

Maternity/Paternity

In some countries, maternity and paternity leave may be legally required, but fathers may receive nothing, depending on the country, and will need to use vacation hours to assist the mother. We can't use sick hours because we are not sick. The number of weeks allowed for mothers varies, so we should check our employee handbook or with HR.

Retirement

Unless an employer is tiny or new, they offer retirement plans. Younger people new to the corporate world sometimes ignore these, but this is a mistake due to compound interest. This means that the interest we earn on our deposits is added back to our balance and also earns interest. This can add up significantly. Our employer will explain the details of this during orientation and it pays to listen. Even a little contribution now can have a huge return by the time we need it.

Companies typically match a percentage of our contribution. They are literally giving us money for doing it. But there's a catch known as vesting. This means whether we get to keep their contributions, and how much. A common scenario is that for each year of employment, we are more vested than before. If it's a five-year schedule, we might be another 20% vested with each year. After five years, we keep 100% of the employer's share of contributions. This also adds up. Frequently switching jobs before this vesting milestone can be costly to our retirement account.

Some employers, or the retirement planning firm they use, have limits. For example, we may be unable to contribute for 3-6 months. Or we can start on the first day of the first full month of employment. This is something to ask during our discussions with HR during the hiring phase, though there is nothing they can do about it. Still, it is nice to know, and we may use it as a bargaining chip for a higher salary if we can't contribute for a long time.

When we leave jobs, we can also leave a trail of retirement accounts behind us. These accumulating accounts become harder to manage or keep track of. It's wise to hire a financial advisor who can set up our own accounts. Then we can move our funds from a now-former employer to our self-managed one. Or we can move funds to our new employer. For consultants and contractors, having our own is wise because we cannot otherwise get one.

Training

Some companies provide training by sending us to a course that is anywhere from a half day to five full days in a single week. The vendor may supply lunch, cookies, and drinks, plus the course materials. Training is typically on a computer in a room full of other students, but we can do them virtually today as well. That we attend is usually all that matters to our employer. While tests may exist, scores are not necessarily reported back to our boss. Find out.

This training can be mandatory and come with a catch—they pay the entire bill (usually over $1500), but if we leave the company within a year of the course, we have to pay them back, meaning they take the cost from our final paycheck. This is one reason to ensure the training is something our career would truly benefit from. This is not always easy because the vendors may be restricted and the course offerings may not genuinely interest us. If the training is not mandatory but encouraged, they may pressure us to do it and could see declining as a hint that we are considering leaving the company, so be careful with this.

CHAPTER FOURTEEN

Finding Jobs

Whether or not we already have a job, several issues arise when trying to find another.

First, a quick word about interviews. We should strive to moderate how much we talk. Some people say too little while others talk too much from nervousness. Neither makes a good impression. We can also talk ourselves out of a job more easily the more we speak. In an extreme example, I once interviewed a man who spoke so much that me and my team only asked him three questions during the hour-long meeting. We were unable to ask most of what we wanted to know, he told us many things we did not care about, and none of us wanted to work with someone who talked so much. But it could be an effective strategy to give longer answers during a verbal technical exam because they may not get to ask us as many questions. Time dictates these exams more than a set number of inquiries.

Job Searching

When actively looking via job boards, it helps to keep our resume near the top of search results when recruiters are looking for candidates. The way to achieve this is by logging in every Sunday night, or Monday morning, and making a trivial change, such as adding a space somewhere, and then saving it. This will show that we just updated our resume and must therefore be actively looking by Monday morning, when they search. They often sort the results by the date of last update; this may be the default order. The calls and emails to us will rise this week, but for each week that we do not do this, they will fall again. Not updating our account this way will create the impression that we are not actively looking, but we will still be contacted, just not as often.

Once we have landed a new job, some of us deactivate our resume so that it doesn't appear in the searches and these contacts stop. It may be wiser to just leave it alone. Employers do not expect us to deactivate it once hired, so there is no risk to our current job for leaving it up. Recruiters regularly take candidate information from the job boards and enter or update them in their company's database, and in time, our resume will increasingly spread, but not as much if we hide it. When they are looking for candidates, they check not only the boards, but their database of existing contacts, even if we have never communicated with them directly before. This is one reason even deactivating the resume will not stop the contacts, and why would we want to?

Because responding can be time-consuming. And some recruiters won't take no for an answer. But we do not have to respond. Some will say it is rude not to, but not receiving a response is a fact of modern life. And there are many instances when a recruiter contacts us, we write back, and they do not respond again. This is a two-way street. Either all of us are required to respond every time, or none of us are. It is the latter. But it's good to have a prepared response that we copy and paste. Something like:

Thank you for your email. I am not currently looking but have attached a current resume. I specialize in XYZ and 123. I am usually seeking work as Title 1 and Title 2, and I can work from South Location 1 to North Location 2 and over to West Location 3 and East Location 4. I don't foresee relocating and the option to telework X number of days per week is attractive to me.

This tells them much of what they need to know to categorize us and reach out when they hopefully have something on target. Save salary information for when they respond (if they do).

Recruiters often contact us when they arguably shouldn't. We can indicate that we won't relocate and still receive jobs halfway across the country. We can say we will only do employment and be contacted about contracting jobs. Only full-time and get part-time. If we are in technology, they can contact us about jobs for skills that are nowhere on our resume and yet the job description says we need years of experience. These are the contacts and recruiters that may have a lower requirement for responding. Early in our careers, we might mind this less, but as the years pass, this can change.

It is wise to keep most contact via email unless we are interested in a position. The reason is recruiter persistence. Sometimes we tell them we are not interested and yet cannot get off the phone for twenty minutes. They want to know many things that may be obvious from our resume, and other items we can tell them in under sixty seconds, but they keep wanting to talk. If we work in a hot field and job market, we might end up on the phone for hours a day to discuss positions we don't want. Many of the calls come while we're at work and can't talk, worsening this problem.

Be careful with updating an active/viewable resume if employed. Our employer's recruiters can see us in the search results and will reach the same conclusion as all recruiters—we must be actively looking for another job. They may be required to tell the HR Director and our manager, maybe a Vice President. Many people have been fired for this. It is not a myth (it happened to me twice in a row). If we want to update the resume but are not looking, then we need to either make it anonymous or deactivate it. I suggest saving the changes until intending to depart. The online version of our resume isn't the official one, so just update that real one and leave the online copies alone until then. This allows recruiters to continue finding us.

Some job boards allow us to be "anonymous." This means our identifying information, including name, and our current employer, is hidden when recruiters look at our resume. While this protects us, it also seems to reduce the number of contacts we receive. It also lessens the likelihood of our information being added to their database because they don't know who we are. In the past, one job board allowed us to choose our current employer from a list and block their recruiters from seeing our resume, which was not anonymous. Sadly, this feature vanished a decade ago.

There are several likely reasons companies can let us go on discovering we are looking for another job. Spite is one. Managers sometimes take it personally, like we are rejecting them. And maybe we are. If we don't have a good relationship with them, they may do this. That we want to leave can suggest that our manager is not doing a good job of managing us and they are the problem, so they invent reasons to fire us, putting the blame on us. Some employers assume an unhappy staff member will be unproductive. Others may have been considering downsizing, possibly over budget issues, and we just volunteered ourselves.

We usually will not understand our employer has discovered our intent to leave until they call us into a meeting and unceremoniously fire us for it; they usually admit this is the reason because they feel justified. Some are triumphant, like they caught us and they want us to know they are smarter than us, and we haven't fooled them. It is odd watching someone be immature while acting superior.

If we want to leave but have a good relationship with our manager, and we want to discuss it with them, we can do so, but proceed with caution. They can tell someone else who has different ideas. Our relationship with them might also not be what we thought it was. Unless we have a pressing *need* to tell them before resigning, we should not. The risk isn't worth it. Companies, and this includes our manager and HR, will always say they are there to support us, but it is the other way around. We are there to support them, and once it becomes clear we don't intend to, we are not a partner in their success. Some will consider us a potential threat to it either through actual malfeasance or implied indifference to their goals.

Recruiters

Recruiters specialize in finding and contacting prospective employees for a company. There are arguably two types: those who are trying to find employees to join the staff of the company for which they work, and those who seek staff for a different company. The latter may freelance but they typically work at recruiting firms, who are hired by companies that may not have a dedicated staff to do this work. They may have a few recruiters but outsource the process anyway or augment it. It doesn't really matter to us as a prospective employee.

Recruiters usually get our contact information from a job board, a job fair, or from the company's database. How they got it is irrelevant unless we are curious what is working for us. If there are three job boards but everyone contacts us because of one of them, we know where to spend our energy. If we ask, explain this is why we are asking. If we only ask, "Where did you get my information?" this can come across as challenging and make them feel defensive—and like we are not civil. Instead, ask, "Can you tell me where you got my info? I'm curious which job boards are working for me." And when they tell us, we thank them.

If we indicate our preference for being contacted, such as via email or phone, recruiters often ignore this, maybe to do whatever works best for them. It's still worth indicating our preference. They may email, call, and text, in which case we should respond via the medium that works best for us. If interested in the position, the phone is recommended for speed of exchanging information and assessing the opportunity. If we are not interested, email keeps this from taking too much of our time. Texting has the advantage of being less formal while maintaining the same distance as email, but there is an expectation that we will respond more quickly once interaction has begun.

Some recruiters will give us a significant amount of information in their first contact, particularly by email. They will say where the job is located, meaning the city, and if they're hiring directly for their company or they work for a recruiting firm, whether it's full time, contract, if corp-to-corp is allowed. They will send the job title and a full job description. These are golden. Others will only write that they have a job and to respond if interested, as if they did anything to get us interested. In between these extremes is everyone else, and we can tell how good they are, and maybe even how interested in us they are, by the quality of their approach.

With recruiting firms, more than one may contact us for the same job. If Company 1 has no recruiters, they may exclusively contract a recruiting firm to find someone. Or they will publicly post the job, which allows all recruiting firms to see it and try to find candidates. It is not uncommon to hear about the same job from five different recruiters, two of whom may work for the same firm! Sometimes they ask us if others have approached us about the position before, or even if we have been submitted for it. Be honest and stick with the first recruiter unless there is a significant problem, including hearing bad things about the recruiting company, or a previous unpleasant experience with them.

Some recruiters will share no information about the job until they get us on the phone. They can make it clear by repeated refusals to answer questions, and some will even admit it. Whether this is their idea or their employer's, this is uncooperative. Unless we are desperate, we do not need to accept this, and since we do not know what job they have in mind, maybe we are not losing much; we'll never know, at any rate, unless we submit to this.

Recruiters will explain the interview process and are usually correct about the non-technical part of it. For software developers or others who might be subjected to a technical exam, they are often wrong, though they are trying. We can be told there is no exam and get an intensive one and vice versa. Sometimes they tell us what the exam covers and are completely wrong. We might be told the format is verbal when it's a computer test, or handwritten, or even writing on a chalkboard. These can make it hard to prepare. Recruiters are apologetic when they learn of the mistake, and they genuinely appreciate it when we tell them what the test actually entailed; this makes it easier for them to tell the next candidate. This doesn't directly help us, but it improves good will toward us, should they contact us again.

Another element recruiters often get wrong is how long the interview will be. This can be problematic if our car is in metered parking and it runs overtime, for example. Or if we left our car with a garage valet and told him we would be back in two hours and are there in one; now he must shuffle more cars than he was expecting to retrieve our vehicle.

Some recruiting firms have a policy that requires meeting us in person, or more recently via video, before they can send us to interview with their client. This can be a disadvantage and is uncommon enough in the U.S. that we can decline if we have enough other opportunities. Some will acknowledge that this is inconvenient and explain that they consider it one benefit they offer their clients. But it does not offer us the same benefit. While we must meet them, another recruiting firm that doesn't have this requirement may have sent another candidate to interview already, and they were offered the job while our recruiter was still "benefitting" us by interviewing us in person first. We must often take time off from work to do this as well.

Sometimes these meetings take place in a restaurant, which implies we'll be having a meal, or at least a snack, but this isn't a given. It's smart to eat light ahead of this and then order light if food is ordered, partly so that we aren't stuffing our face. Declining altogether is a refusal of their hospitality, so at least find an appetizer. Under no circumstances we will pay for their portion, but they will probably pay for ours. Some will proactively tell us when the check comes, but we may prefer to pull out our wallet until they wave us off, as it is better than an assumption that turns out to be wrong; this is awkward. Besides, the certainty feels better and provides an chance to thank them.

Networking is often discussed as a kind of Holy Grail of job hunting. There is some truth to this, but it is overstated. The odds are not great that a recruiter we have spoken to before will have a job that fits all of our criteria at the precise moment that we are looking to change jobs. Plenty of recruiters we have never spoken to will contact us anyway, so it is not like we depend on having networked with them. Some people are not good at this or dislike it, but worry that they must do it. This is not true. It can depend on our profession, the job market, and experience. Given how many recruiters and firms exist, we may consider it a desire more than a necessity.

Determine Our Market Value

Determining our market value can confuse us, especially early in our careers. Some job postings will admit the salary along with the details that presumably cause it, but that doesn't mean we qualify based on our experience. We might get $50k for it while someone else gets $60k. There is a simple way to get feedback that is tailored to us and our resume. We tell the recruiter what we want and judge the reaction, of which there are three.

Immediately and enthusiastically accepting our number means we probably should have asked for more. This may be why they sound thrilled and confident they can approve that salary request; they do not have to ask their manager. We lowballed ourselves. They will have found a skilled candidate for less money than someone else. They will look good to their supervisor. This response is noteworthy and attention grabbing for what seems like encouragement that can lift our hope of landing the job, but we should be crestfallen on hearing it.

Examples of this response:

- "We can definitely do that."
- "Absolutely!"
- "Oh sure, that's not a problem at all."
- "Of course! We'd be happy to do that."

At the other extreme is the immediate rejection. This means we are thousands above the known maximum and there is little to no chance of getting it. We have, in this moment, potentially cost ourselves the position, and this is precisely why many people are afraid to ask for more money. However, we can salvage this with an appropriate reaction to their response, examples of which include:

- "Umm. Do you have any wiggle room?"
- "Well, the most we can do for this position is XXX. Would you be able to do that?"
- "I'm sorry, we can't go that high."
- "Oh, well, um, I can ask. I might have to talk to the hiring manager."
- "Oh, you might be a little too senior/experienced for the role."
- "I don't think we can do that for this role, but we get positions that are closer to that if you would like to be kept in mind."

All we need to do is say that we have room to come down a bit, and that salary is not the only thing we consider. We can mention the commute, benefits, the potential longevity of the position, and more. The goal is to sound reasonable and flexible, and that we are open to less money depending on circumstances. Then we should ask what they can offer. This talk about money is almost always in the initial call, long before we learn far more details, so we try to position ourselves as willing to consider the job anyway depending on what else we learn during the interview process. Most recruiters will continue the conversation if everything else was going well before this. They do not hang up and are rarely rude. They still want to be civil, be professional, and network, at the least.

In between these reactions is the one we will most often receive—acceptance with no particular enthusiasm. We may get no reaction at all as they move on to another subject, though they have likely jotted it down. This tells us we are in the ballpark and not at either extreme, but it also suggests we might get away with asking for more. The question is how much? Examples of this response include:

- "Okay."
- "Sure, we can do that."
- "We can make that work."
- "Not a problem."

The question everyone has is—how do we determine our market value without asking for too much money and costing ourselves a job? The answer is to ask for the highest amount of money we think we can make, but do it with jobs that we already know we don't want for whatever reason—and gauge the reaction. That way, we cost ourselves nothing and get to evaluate the response.

For example, we currently make $50k and think we can make $60k. A job we want calls and we're afraid to lose it by asking $60k so we only ask for $55k, or maybe still

$50k. They immediately accept and we know we went too low. Now we'll be stuck with it if we get hired.

The other scenario is that a recruiter calls about a job we soon realize we do not want under any circumstances. They ask our salary and we toss out $60k and evaluate the response. Immediate acceptance means that if another recruiter calls for a similar job, we ask for $65k. If they immediately reject $60k, maybe $60k is indeed on the top end. If the response is more moderate, we now know we should probably make $60k but could go higher to $65k before getting the immediate rejection. Now we know our market value, and we risked nothing to find out, just jobs we didn't want anyway.

Every job and employer is different. Some of them pay a lot and some pay little. We have to repeat this experiment with a dozen recruiters while paying attention to overall compensation and the details of what the job is asking us to do. With repetition, we can determine our market value.

The Past Salary Question

Many of us are afraid to ask for more money than what we currently make, because we expect being asked to justify that; the bigger the gap, the more this is true. But if they don't know what we are currently making, this worry goes away.

We do not have to tell them our current salary. Increasingly, states are enacting laws to prohibit employers from asking past salary information. An updated list of such jurisdictions in the United States is maintained at this link: http://bit.ly/SalaryBanUSStates. These bans often include forbidding employers asking us directly or contacting former employers to ask. If a salary ban covers our location, we can stop worrying about it.

For everyone else, they may verbally ask us. I always respond to this question with what I am looking to make now, as if I didn't hear the question right. Few will ask us again but if so, I just repeat, "I'm looking to make XXX." If they try to insist, we can reply that we consider this personal information and we do not give it out. We are not alone in being unwilling to grant the request, so they have heard such responses before.

If a job application lists salary, we do not have to fill it in even if they observe that we skipped it. We can respond that we don't give that information out. They may insist, and when we are younger, we may accept this and provide it. Our past salary is a "nice to have" piece of information on us, not a true requirement. Ultimately, it is not their business, though we should not say this. By the time they are asking, they have often given us a job offer (which includes salary) that they will not rescind just because we omit this.

Some companies have a policy forbidding giving out salary information to anyone calling and asking for it, but we seldom know this. We would need to ask HR, and it is a question best asked during onboarding so that it doesn't look like we are considering leaving.

Understanding why employers ask helps us navigate the situation. They want to see if we have been steadily increasing our salary because this suggests we have done well and are ambitious enough to do great work, rather than lounge around, as a flat salary history might suggest. In other words, they are going to interpret the numbers to mean something, but people read different things into this. That makes it hard to know what they are really getting at. We can ask, "What is it you want to know about me from my salary history?" They may not want to answer because we can just respond by telling them what they want to hear. It is a cat-and-mouse game best handled with a smile. We have the upper hand. In the end, they want to know that we are serious about our career and taking charge, so we can impart this with the maturity and certainty with which we conduct our negotiations—and the polite kindness that we use while denying the request for our salary history.

Conclusion

The corporate world is much like any other—it is what we make of it. I hope this book has helped you understand some nuances that await and which can cause unforeseen problems. These are the issues that pose an obstacle that can disillusion us and make us decide that maybe this world isn't right for us after all. My goal is not to convince you to stay against your best wishes, but to help you hurdle these on your race to greater happiness in your career.

Remember to be true to yourself and your goals, and loyal to both. The days of loyalty to an employer were two generations ago for most people and not expected anymore. When our interests and those of the company diverge, we should be honest with ourselves about our time there and decide where our next best option lies. And then find it on our terms.

If you enjoyed reading my anecdotes, I enjoy such tales myself. Email me your own stories at mail@randy-zinn.com. While I can't give advice because I won't know enough about your situation, I can certainly offer an understanding ear. I have two forthcoming books, *Corporate Hell: A Memoir,* and *Consulting Hell: A Memoir*, that cover most of my time in this world. Keep an eye out for them if you need a good laugh and to see that you are not alone in dealing with unexpected surprises.

Work better, sooner.

———— ● · ● ————

If you enjoyed this book, more Randy Zinn memoirs are available at https://amzn.to/2XZWwFw or use the QR code below:

About the Author

Randy Zinn has worked as a software developer/architect in the Washington D.C. area for over 20 years as an employee, contractor, or consultant through his own company. He's a proud father to a son (b. 2012) and daughter (b. 2016) and loves spending time with them when not writing fiction, making music, playing golf, or exercising. Under another name, he's published non-fiction and fantasy novels, and released several albums of his music (hard rock and acoustic guitar). He holds a Bachelor of Music in classical guitar, Magna cum Laude.

He's also faced a variety of personal issues, including Inattentive ADHD, speech problems, depression, bullying, being Learning Disabled, and a crippling injury, all of which he overcame. His memoirs cover these and his life-changing transformation.

Connect with me online

http://www.Randy-Zinn.com
https://www.facebook.com/pg/randyzinnauthor
http://bit.ly/ZinnAmazon

If you like this book, please help others enjoy it.

Lend it. Please share this book with others.
Recommend it. Please recommend it to friends, family, reader groups, and discussion boards

Review it. Please review the book at Goodreads and the vendor where you bought it.

JOIN THE RANDY ZINN NEWSLETTER!

Subscribers receive a FREE eBook of *Adventures in Opposite Land (The Memoir Shorts, 1)*! You also get a chance to join the ARC team and see books before they're published.

http://www.randy-zinn.com/newsletter

Randy Zinn Books

MEMOIRS

Corporate Hell: A Memoir
Consulting Hell: A Memoir

A Storm of Lies: A Father's Fight to Raise His Children

A Silence Not So Golden Trilogy
Book 1: *Refusal to Engage: My Voice is Become Death*
Book 2: *A Blast of Light: My Rebirth Through Music*
Book 3: *The Wine-Dark Sea: My New Life Awaits*

The Memoir Shorts
Book 1: *Adventures in Opposite Land*
Book 2: *Am I Evil?*

OTHER NON-FICTION

The Corporate Life Survival Guide

View all books at Amazon: